School Social Workers

About the Author

Arti Mann has earned her Ph.D. from IGNOU, New Delhi. Her professional interest remains in the area of women, children, guidance and counselling, and juvenile delinquency.

Arti Mann has participated in large number of seminars and conferences, and has published several research papers and articles in well known journals. She has accomplished various certificate courses like on HIV/AIDS, Self-Help Group etc. from IGNOU, New Delhi. She has also completed a short-term certificate course in guidance and counselling from Delhi University.

School Social Workers

Roles and Contributions in Child Learning

Arti Mann

CONCEPT PUBLISHING COMPANY PVT. LTD.
NEW DELHI-110059

ISBN-13: 978-93-5125-122-4

First Published 2018

Published and Printed by

Concept Since 1974

Concept Publishing Company Pvt. Ltd.
A/15-16, Commercial Block, Mohan Garden
New Delhi-110059 (India)
T: 25351460, 25351794, *F*: 091-11-25357109
E: publishing@conceptpub.com, W: www.conceptpub.com

Cataloging in Publication Data—Courtesy: D.K. Agencies (P) Ltd. < docinfo@dkagencies.com >

Mann, Arti, author.
School social workers : roles and contributions in child learning / Arti Mann.
pages cm
Includes bibliographical references and index.
ISBN 9789351251224

1. School social work—India—Delhi. 2. Students—Mental health services—India—Delhi. I. Title.

LCC LB1027.5.M36 2018 DDC 371.460954 23

Acknowledgements

Reaching at the stage where I am today, would not have been possible if I did not have the untiring and continuous support from a number of persons. It is the time to look back and recognize the efforts put by each and every person who has immensely contributed in the book presented here. It gives me immense pleasure to record my gratitude and appreciation to those who has directly and indirectly contributed in developing this book.

My heartiest gratitude to my supervisors, Prof. Gracious Thomas and Dr. Archana Kaushik for their invaluable scholarly suggestions. I am greatly thankful to both of them for being utmost supportive and patient throughout my work. Their immense intellect and attention towards minute details helped me during my work to reach a successful end. I am indebted to my guides throughout my life for their extreme supportive attitude.

I greatly acknowledge the support and guidance provided by Dr. G. Mahesh (Ph.D. Coordinator, IGNOU) for his continuous appreciation, support and guidance throughout the work.

I would also like the opportunity to thank teachers, staff, students and their parents of various schools for sparing their precious time, experience, feelings and ideas. Without their cooperation the work would not be successfully accomplished.

I especially thanks with bottom of my heart to all authorities who allow me to collect relevant information for the work.

I offer my sincere gratitude and appreciation to Mr. Ashok Kumar Mittal, Managing Director of Concept Publishing Company Pvt. Ltd., for his guidance and encouragement. It is largely due to his efforts, boundless enthusiasm and dedication that the book was brought out in record time.

My thanks are also due to my parents Sh. Ajit Singh Mann

(father) and Smt. Kamlesh (mother) and my elder brother Mr. Praveen Kumar for their moral and emotional support. Their constant encouragement kept me motivated to complete my work.

I am particularly grateful to my husband Mr. Pawan Kumar for his continuous support in typing the manuscript and the encouragement provided by him during the period.

I am also grateful to my in-laws Sh. Ishwar Singh Phogat (father-in-law) and Smt. Basanti Devi (mother-in-law) and my beloved children, Vivaan Phogat and Vedant Phogat for understanding my work pressure and keeping me free from domestic work and allowing me to execute the work satisfactorily.

Towards the last but definitely not the least, I would like to thanks all my relatives and friends for supporting me throughout my journey.

New Delhi **Arti Mann**

Contents

List of Tables

List of Figures

Abbreviations

CCE	Continuous and Comprehensive Evaluation
CGC	Child Guidance Clinic
DoE	Directorate of Education
DEWO	Divisional Education Welfare Officer
DMC	Delhi Municipal Committee
DSSW	Delhi School of Social Work
DU	Delhi University
ESAA	Emergency School Aid Act
ESEA	Elementary and Secondary Education Act
ETE	Elementary Teacher Education
EWO	Education Welfare Officer
EWS	Economic Weaker Section
FA	Formative Assessment
HoD	Head of Department
IATSW	Indian Association of Trained Social Workers
IGNOU	Indira Gandhi National Open University
ITI	Industrial Training Institute
JBT	Junior Basic Training
LDC	Lower Division Clerk
MCD	Municipal Corporation of Delhi
NASW	National Association of Social Worker
NCERT	National Council of Educational Research &Training
NDMC	New Delhi Municipal Council
NGO	Non-Governmental Organisation

OBC	Other Backward Class
PGT	Post-Graduate Teacher
PPSS	Pune Palak Shikshak Sangh
PTA	Parent-Teacher Association
SARD	Society for All Round Development
SC	Scheduled Caste
ST	Scheduled Tribe
SSA	Sarva Shiksha Abhiyan
SUPW	Socially Useful and Productive Work
TISS	Tata Institute of Social Sciences
TGT	Trained Graduate Teacher
UDC	Upper Division Clerk
UEE	Universal Elementary Education
UK	United Kingdom
USA	United States of America
WHO	World Health Organisation

1
Origin of School-based Social Work Programme

Introduction

The human child comes into the world as a biological organism. Then he or she is gradually moulded in society into a social being and learns social ways of behaving and interacting with fellow beings. Through the process of socialization, this biological being is 'transformed' into social-being. Family and school have been taken as the primary agents of socialization, having profound influence on the personality of the individual. The process of socialization begins with the family first where the child develops 'identity' and 'self-concept'. School-system is the second most prominent agency of socialization, which plays a vital role in development of a child's psyche, attitudes, values and personality predispositions. Thus, the family and the school are the central places for the development of children. Children are born as '*tabula-rasa*' (or blank slate) and socialization agents like families and schools, imprint knowledge, perceptions, values and attitudes that guide the behaviours throughout the life time (*see* Locke, cited in Russell, 1994).

As maintained by Nelson Mandela, "education is the most powerful weapon which you can use to change the world". It signifies the vital role of education and importance of schools or educational institutions. The purpose of schooling is the transmission of culture, the process by which the culture of a society is passed on to its children. As one of the most stable and formal socializing agent, the school is expected to both train the individual for practical occupations and skills and to provide with basic societal values, like respect to elders, obeying civic norms etc. (Saldana, 2013).

Among several professionals working in the school system, one of them is social worker, who is equipped with various skills, principles, methods and scientific knowledge. The social workers with these skills can play an important role in the personality growth of the student.

To understand the role and functioning of the social worker, it is necessary to examine the functioning of the school.

Importance of School

Henslin (1999) states, that schools are the agents responsible for socializing groups of children and young people on specific skills and values in a society. The school system has become the glue that holds the society together by bringing dynamism as well as acting as a stabilizer. It probably contributes most to social conformity (Appelbaum and Chambliss, 1997). The school system responds to society's needs, and complies with society's demands, for trained workers, intellectual and well-educated citizens (Saldana, 2013).

Counts (1932) has commented, "we are convinced that education is the one unfailing remedy for every ill to which man is subject, whether it be vice, crime, war, poverty, riches, injustice, racketeering, political corruption, race hatred, class conflict, or just plain original sin. We even speak glibly and often about the general reconstruction of society through the school." In the contemporary world, schools are expected to teach young minds knowledge and expertise for career, life-skills, value education, conflict resolution, and sex education. Thus, education is becoming all-encompassing and the role of school is expanding.

In the Indian system, the school education is divided into three levels—

1. Primary level,
2. Middle level, and
3. Secondary level.

At primary level, the child is explored with various basic concepts in pictorial form so that it will impress long-lasting impression on their mind. During this stage more stress is given on the motor development of the child by encouraging and motivating them.

In middle school, in addition to the academic input the child is more involved with peer group and other co-curricular activities and shows interest in various things to explore their talents.

After middle school comes secondary stage, at this stage cognitive development becomes more specific and the students are taught according to the interest or in the area which is more suited to their aptitude.

All this shows that schools provide plenty of opportunities to the children to habituate themselves in moral ideal just like family. Seemingly, it is true that schools "undo developmental deficiencies caused by familial socialization process" (Robinson, 1978).

There are many reasons why schools are given so much importance today, salient ones are stated below:

Now-a-days, joint family systems are giving way to smaller units like nuclear families. In ancient and medieval times, joint families and extended families played many significant roles including provision of education, life-skills, moral education, inculcating values. However, in the present times, most of these roles have been taken-up by other agencies outside the family system (Kaushik, 2005). And, the school system became the primary source of imparting education to the children. Other than providing technical education or vocational training, schools are playing significant role in imparting values, perceptions and life-skills, which traditionally have been the scope of roles of families, particularly grand-parents.

In the contemporary globalized world, the role of parents is shrinking, especially in providing moral values or emotional support, especially when both the parents are engaged in economic pursuits outside home. Adults in parental role are undergoing various kinds of social, psychological and economical pressures. As a result, to overcome these pressures, parents have to work harder and for longer duration. This leaves them with very little time for socialization of their children. Children, at a very young age, are sent to crèches and play schools. A few decades back, a child would go to school after attaining five years of age, but now trend has changed and children are initiated into school system as early as at two years or even younger. This is because of change in the lifestyle of people. For instance, more women now prefer to be gainfully employed over their roles in home-making and parenting. Therefore, parents need to make some arrangement for the child care and early initiation into school system is their preferred choice. Parental pre-occupation with their jobs, reducing family size, loneliness, none to care and share and such other factors are resulting into increased sense of anxiety, stress and insecurities among the children. Schools offer the scope of fulfilling this gap between parent-child communication and interactions.

However, shrinking role of family system has put additional responsibilities on the school system. How the schools are coping with these surplus tasks and duties? Are the teachers overburdened or school authorities have employed additional staff like psychiatrists, psychologists and social workers, other than teachers to accomplish these tasks?

Educationists have stressed that for optimum development of children there should be strong inter-linkage between the school system and the parents or families. Social workers working in the school setting are the connecting link (Robinson, 1978). Often times, there are gaps in the relationship of the pupil with his/her school or within the family or between the school and the family—all these affect the development of children. The gaps between the school system and the family have repercussions on gaining benefits of education. Social workers have been professionally trained to fill-in these gaps in the school setting.

School social workers are an integral link between school, home, and community in helping students achieve academic success. They work directly with the pupils having problems in adjusting in their social environment, coping with studies, anxiety, issues related to developmental tasks, scholastic backwardness, truancy, school phobia. Social workers deal with school administration as well as students and families and facilitate school system in achieving its objectives. School social workers play wide range of roles preventive, management, supportive, promotive, mental health intervention, crises-management and support services. As part of an inter-disciplinary team to help students succeed, social workers also facilitate community involvement in the schools while advocating for student success.

School Social Work Association of America (2009) maintains that school social work is a specialized area of practice within the broad field of the social work profession. School social workers bring unique knowledge and skills to the school system and the student services team. They are instrumental in furthering the purpose of the schools to provide a setting for teaching, learning, and for the attainment of competence and confidence. They are appointed by school authorities to enhance the school's ability to meet its academic mission, especially when home, school and community collaboration is the key to achieving that mission.

Across the globe, schools are increasingly becoming the main public institution for social development. Earlier the educational institutions in the traditional societies used to provide the knowledge to select few. Education was not the right of all the children but the privilege that only few elite families could afford for their children. Now-a-days, schools are aiming to make the social order more egalitarian and based on equality. Thus, schools are working towards including the traditionally disadvantaged children (based on caste, class, and gender), who were excluded from the opportunity of education. They are raising standards for educational outcomes to prepare citizens to participate in a multi-cultural world, where diversity is respected and which is bound by rights based approach.

In this situation, the school social worker is becoming a useful professional to assist children who are marginalized—whether economically, socially, politically, or personally—to participate in the process of empowerment through education. Social workers help in making the education process effective. To do this, their central focus is working in partnership with parents on the pupil in transaction with a complex school and home environment.

In the globalized world, the roles of school social workers are becoming broader and more complex. In a classroom, children from all sections of society, with differential sets of abilities and capabilities, problems and challenges are present. Social work practice rests on a wide range of skills such as counselling, networking, referring, educating, advocating, and so on. School social workers may work one-on-one with teachers, families, and children to address individual situations and needs. They become part of joint efforts to make schools safe and educational process enriching for everyone. There is a scope of school social workers to work with teachers too on their mental health issues, particularly in the light of ever-expanding roles and challenges encountered by the teaching community in the present social setting.

Further, in Indian setting, we do not have common school system. There are private schools and government owned and government aided schools, each type having its own set of strengths and challenges. Government schools, largely caters to children coming from economically weaker sections. Here, the school faces challenges in terms of school dropouts and maintaining quality education. School social workers often have to deal with problems like lack of motivation among parents, no conducive home environment for studies, resistance in sending girl children to school, first generation learning and such others (Gandhi, 1990).

In private schools, with the government's inclusion policy, an increased level of heterogeneity is seen among the pupils of same class and school social workers may encounter problems like bullying, drug addiction, familial problems impacting academic performance, emotional and sexual problems, adjustment with peers from different cultural backgrounds, and so on.

Talking about the status of school social work in India, Gandhi (1990) observes that many social work practitioners and educators have believed that school social work in India has not become a movement and it is still at the experimental stage. The education departments of Central and State Governments have not yet accepted this service as an integral part of their school system. It is only a few private or aided schools in prominent cities which have employed social workers in their schools. The growth achieved so far is attributed to the efforts made by colleges of social work, child guidance clinics, associations of trained social workers, few progressive educationalists and local Parent-Teacher Associations (Gandhi, 1990).

Due to the absence of a close school, home and community liaison, our education system suffers from number of impediments, specific among them are—high dropout rates, mental health problem, adjustment problems, biasness in favour of children from higher socio-economic strata and schools catering for the elite group having no touch with social realities.

Even in contemporary times, there is a debate among the educators and practitioners of social work whether social workers have been able to carve a special place for them in school setting or are still struggling for their identity and recognition. Let us first look at the history of school social work, which would help in analyzing its present status in a better way.

School Social Work : Historical Terrains

To understand a subject thoroughly, its historical and temporal underpinnings need to be appraised meticulously. Hence, holistic appraisal of the field of school social work would be incomplete without understanding its background. The professional social work which we have adopted in India has grown in the United States of America. The education system including the school education which we have in the country was founded by the British. So, it is important to understand the development of school social work in USA and England before understanding its emergence and scope in India.

School Social Work in the USA

School social work in the United States of America (USA) is an integral part of a specialist team of people (psychologists, guidance counsellors, speech therapist etc.) and the team provides school based services. These initiatives initially were taken-up by voluntary agencies in the USA, who usually do home—school liaising. From this initial thrust of providing individualized service the focus gradually shifted to wider tasks like promoting desegregation among race, linking school with family and neighbour and handicapped children's integration in the schools.

The shifting of emphasis led to generating the need of induction of pupil specialist likes psychologists, counsellors, social worker and nurses etc., in the schools. School social workers too got established due to varied reasons. Their post was called as "visiting teachers". The initiation of school social work was made in the year 1906-07 at Hartford, Boston and New York, although factors leading to its establishment at all the places were not uniform. At Hartford, the induction was to prevent the occurrence of mental disorders and this resulted in the establishment of psychological clinics attached to the schools. The school and clinic liaison was essentially a social work task and this was recognized by the appointment of the visiting teachers whereas at New York and Boston the school social worker was included due to the sociological concern in the favour of the disadvantaged children of the settlement.

Miss Mary Marat was the first who initiated this service in New York. She formed a committee along with interested persons. The committee not only financed, but also appointed two visiting teachers in Hartley House and Greenwich House. These teachers were supposed to bring about better understanding between home and school for the benefit of the deprived children of the settlement (Fredricksen, 1948).

At Boston, the Westend Neighbourhood Association, a social settlement, joined hands with the Women's Education Association, a parent-teacher group and appointed a home and school liaison worker (Friedlander, 1963). Here, also the focus was on the poor.

The beginning of school social work, therefore, was made with the realization of making home-school liaison for the full development of school going children. However, the initiative is not taken-up by the schools, but by the private and civil society organizations.

In 1913, the Board of Education, Rochester, New York, accepted the appointment of trained social workers as visiting teachers. This was a breakthrough in the school social work programme. The Board of Education explained—

> "This is the first step in an attempt to meet the need of which the school system has been conscious for some time. It is an undisputed fact that in the environment of the child outside the school is to be found forces which will often times thwart

the school in its endeavours.... The appointment of a visiting teacher is an attempt on the school to meet its responsibility for the whole welfare of the child...and to secure maximum cooperation between the home and the school" (Costin, 1978).

As this was the first government recognition to the work of the visiting teacher. Later on, similar to this, several other parts of the USA appointed the social workers in their schools.

In 1919 the growth and expansion of visiting teachers' movement at national-level gave birth to the Professional Association—National Association of Visiting Teachers. This body published various reports and undertook different surveys etc., in the field of school social work and gave it a different height.

In the year 1921 gradually, Commonwealth Fund got involved in this work and started inviting applications for the demonstration projects for visiting teachers. These projects were based on spreading mental hygiene, increasing focus on children, preventing child delinquency through child guidance services etc. Out of 270 communities-30 communities, whose geographical, social, educational situation found satisfactory, were chosen. And, a visiting teacher was assigned to each community for the period of three years who got permanent on showing valuable performance in their work. They were paid two-thirds of their salary from the Commonwealth Fund and rest one-third from the host community. After three years when the Commonwealth Fund withdrew its support, twenty-one communities continued their work while others integrated their service with schools. As a result by 1930, there were 244 workers working in 31 states (Sikkema, 1951).

With the growing trend of visiting teachers, the National Association of Visiting Teachers gained strength and as a result it started putting extra efforts to popularize the field by establishing high standards of work. With this expansion the focus of the task performed by the visiting teachers started changing from home-school liaison work to case work task with the children. The main reason of this shift was enforcement of Attendance Law and spreading of mental health movement. The enforcement of Attendance Law brought challenges to the school, as children came to school with varied backgrounds. And some of these children came from difficult home situations due to which number of problems arose, which no doubt needed to be tackled individually. On the other hand mental health movement became popular and the visiting teachers were compelled to find answers and develop techniques for the prevention and cure of social maladjustments among school children. All this popularized the case work approach (Costin, 1978).

The depression of 1930s temporarily retarded the growth of visiting teacher. As the depression continued for a long time, the Federal Government introduced programme like supplying food, clothing etc., to the school children in order to support families. And all the work was given to the visiting teachers. As they are pushed into such a situation that it deviate them from their main work but fortunately work, did not get fixed and focus came back to case work with children (Costin, 1978). After depression the case work became popular method to help out children. Costin wrote:

> "If the literature of the period correctly reflects its practice then a transition was fully completed from the earlier focus on school and neighbourhood conditions and social change to a clinical orientation in relations the personality needs of the individual school child" (Costin, 1978).

As the case work in particular and social work in general became popular so in 1945 the "American Association of Visiting Teachers" was renamed to "American Association of School Social Workers". Although, it continued its work for the betterment by improving its quality of social work, raised professional standards and increased the body of knowledge and skills in the field (Sikkema, 1951).

In 1960s the pressure increased to relate the social work service to the national task of gearing the educational programme to suit all school children specially to the needs of economically disadvantaged and children from minority section. A couple of laws which necessitated this change have been passed by the Federal Government from 1965 to 1975.

In 1965, the Elementary and Secondary Education Act (ESEA) was passed due to low performance and high dropout rate among poor children. Thus, in the light of this, compensatory education programmes were provided in order to succeed in high technical society. The Act provided liberal financial assistance for undertaking programme for the improvement of reading and mathematical skills of disadvantaged students. As a result, social workers were involved in identifying disadvantaged children, monitoring their performance, counselling parents, and supporting these children for their education (Denaull, 1978).

Similarly, the Emergency School Aid Act (ESAA) of 1972 encouraged to enroll a substantial proportion of minority group children to reduce minority group isolation and to have concentrated programme to overcome their educational disadvantage for promoting desegregation of various racial and cultural group. As a result, social workers and pupils initiated and implemented activities in which parents and students of different cultural and racial background participated. Except this they also developed parent's groups, in-service training programmes and other programmes for minority children and their families (Mintzies, 1978).

In 1975, the Education for All Handicapped Children Act provided Federal assistance to states for integration of handicapped children in regular educational settings, thereby ensuring their individualized education programme and parental participation in educational decision-making. This necessitated the social worker to make close partnerships with parents and schools for clarifying and advocating the rights of the handicapped children to large community, increasing parents' participation and giving individualized help to the handicapped children and their family (Weatherly, 1978).

With passage of time, social workers enhanced their scope of work to include other issues like malfunctioning of pupils, facilitating liaison between school and community and assessing children's scholastic problems etc. Today social workers form an integral part of the pupil service unit in the United States. In 1975-76 a survey conducted by National Association of Social Worker (NASW), which revealed that fifty out of fifty two State Departments have employed school social workers in their states and the salary of school social workers tend to be the same or higher than that of psychologists, psychiatrics and other professionals of pupil service unit.[1]

The exact number of school social workers is not known, but approximately there are five to seven thousand workers staffed either by school boards or by Federal grants. Together, they all form a strong and big professional group serving children.

School Social Work in England

The school social work[2] service of England is different from that of USA. In England the school children are provided school social work service by two departments—the Education Department and Social Service Department.[3]

The Education Department provides supportive services through its welfare officers. While Social Service Department mainly works for children who have some kind of social vulnerability, both the departments work hand in hand on their well-defined area of operation.

The Education Welfare Officers (EWOs) are the social workers who work under the education department. Initially, they have been taken as untrained social worker with the task of enforcing school attendance. Slowly-slowly, they were dispensed with large number of welfare tasks. With this increase in responsibility the need of trained social workers aroused. The service of trained social worker initially started as a school attendance officer.

According to the Education Act, 1880, attendance was made compulsory thing for the students and it empowered local school boards to prosecute the children and parents for non-attendance. This required a person who could take care of attendance in the schools and that led to appointment of school attendance officers, popularly known as "kid catchers", "whipper in" and "school board men". They had a definite area of operation and visited the houses of long absentees and tried to find out reasons and took necessary actions like convincing parents to send their children to school. They also made vigorous hunts of such children in public places like parks and open spaces etc. (Stuart, 1970).

These officers soon realized that reason of low attendance in school is not only because of parents' carelessness, but the causes are varied in nature like undesirable peer group, authoritarian teachers etc. Because of these different reasons they had to adopt different ways to solve the cases like sometimes liaison with parents and teachers, counselling of children etc. So, they had to perform all these tasks and because of all that the importance of welfare support for school children was soon recognized by the government which resulted into passing of number of educational legislations in the first half of twentieth century (MacMillan, K., n. d).

Some of the prominent Acts may be discussed. The Education Act, 1944 was a significant one. According to this Act local education authorities were made statutorily responsible to provide adequate faculties to all the school going age children of their area like free medical treatment to pupils, mid-day meals etc. This Act also includes children suffering from any "disability of mind and body". For this the local authority had to identify children with special needs to ascertain the educational facilities to them (Education Act, 1944).

The local authorities found school attendance officers more suitable for administrating the new welfare benefits. So, they were opted for the same and renamed as "Education Welfare Officer" (EWO). The EWOs continued to perform their useful role for school going children without being noticed between 1950s and the middle of 1960s.

In 1966, the Bowden Committee organized the importance of the work of EWOs after studying 259 authorities employing 2000 EWOs. The Committee, however, was not satisfied with the existing EWOs. As according to the Committee most of the time of EWOs was spent on doing clerical work, dispensing school meals, taking school attendance etc. The Committee stated that, "It is not satisfactory that the service responsible for welfare work in connection with school children should be largely untrained" (Plowden Report, n. d). So, the committee emphasized on the type of work and need of trained social worker. The implication of the report if applied, were that either the EWOs would go for in service social work training or hand over their jobs to trained social worker. As a result they themselves handed over their jobs to trained social worker and they worked as welfare assistants but this degraded their service and also made them feel that they were being imparted step motherly treatment. And they nicknamed their service as "Cinderella Service" (MacMillan, K., n. d).

Then Seebohm Committee came into existence, which also stressed on the need for social work training for EWOs. Along with it also suggested that the social workers should not confine their work just to home and school liaison, but should also look into all general problems related to the children and the concerned families and they should be placed as generic social workers in social service department (Seebohm Report, 1968). But in between the EWOs who were so far operating from Education Department opposed to their merger with social service. As a result the legislation which followed the Seebohm Committee left it to the discretion of each local authority whether they would like to provide their welfare service through the education department or from the proposed social service department. In 1971 when social service department was established only few like Cheshire, Coventry, Devon and Somerset chose to get merged, while other kept on operating through Education Department (MacMillan, K., n. d).

Then Lincoln Ralph Committee came, which gave fairly comprehensive picture of EWOs work and strongly recommended social work training for them. Because of that the EWOs gradually started coming forward for social work training as their work is being recognized among professional groups. Several young qualified people started joining this service.

EWOs at present operate under different organizational models of service in Education Department to meet the local needs. They usually consist of the following team of professionals:

- *Divisional Education Welfare Officer (DEWO)*—To supervise the work of following officers and responsible for day-to-day activities—
  - Deputy Divisional Education Welfare Officer.
  - Assistant Divisional Educational Welfare Officer.
  - Senior Divisional Educational Welfare Officer.
  - Education Welfare Officer.
  - School Care Workers (the voluntary workers who assist EWOs).
  - Child Moral Welfare Officers (all cases of molestation, moral danger and pregnancy among school girls are referred to them).

Although EWOs carried out various tasks in accordance with local needs, but are similar in their main functional areas. The functions of EWOs founded by the Ralph Committee were related to the following:

- Free meal dispersions
- Clothing
- Transport
- School attendance
- Child development
- Child ignorance
- Maintenance
- Catering needs of handicapped children
- Court proceedings
- Placement of children.

And the future roles of EWOs which are recommended by the committee have been as follows:

- Assessing the social, educational and emotional problem of child which affects the children's ability like behavioural problems, poverty, mental and physical handicap etc.
- Developing good relations between teacher, children, and parents so that it can help them to solve their problems.
- Locate resources and utilize them properly.
- Case referencing to the various department or agencies between teachers, children and parents.
- Enforcement of law and legislation.
- Assisting in section and allocation of children to nursery schools and classes.

The Social Service Department

The other department through which the social work services flow to the school children is the social service department. It also came into existence in 1971, the department followed Seebohm Committee recommendations. These agencies carry out comprehensive services in the field of welfare, health nursing and education through trained social workers for the children and their families who are at risk.

Organizational set-up of these agencies are as follows:

- Director of Social Services
- Assistance Director
- Senior Workers
- Social Workers

Social Workers are empowered with statutory powers to conduct social service task through Children Act of 1948, Children and Young Persons Act of 1963 and 1969.

They performed various tasks for the school children.[4] Section 1 of Children Act of 1948, lay down that any child under 17 can be taken into care where there are two parents or guardians or where he or she is prevented from being provided adequate care and likewise they could also entrust the responsibility of the child to the social service department for one or several reasons mentioned below:

(a) If proper development of child is being prevented or neglected.
(b) If he/she is exposed to moral danger.
(c) If he/she is of compulsory school age and is not receiving full-time education suitable to his/her age, ability and aptitude.
(d) If he/she is guilty of an offense excluding homicide and also that he/she is in need of care or control which he/she is unlikely to receive unless the Court makes an order.

Section 1 of Children Young Person Act of 1963, broaden the scope of social services for the children by stating that "they are empowered to make any provision of kind or cash in order to prevent children from being received in care or being in care."

The Children and Young Person Act of 1969 makes it obligatory to inform the Director of Social Services for the persons bringing care proceeding to Juvenile Court. In hearing case proceedings and matrimonial proceedings the Court may decide to make supervision under to the local authority. This means that the child may be supervised in his own home by the social workers of Social Service Department.

The overall functioning of Social Services Department in connection with school children are as follows:

(a) Providing advice, guidance and assistance for the welfare of children.
(b) Providing community homes of various kinds.
(c) Accepting certain children into care and be responsible for their welfare and care.
(d) Investigating allegations of cruelty and neglect.
(e) Providing day care including the children less than five years of age.

School social work service in England is still flowing from its sources namely education department and social service department, but the debates are also continuing about the location of most suitable model for the operation of social work in school.

School Social Work in India

School social work in India is still in the nascent phase where it has to prove its relevance in the education system. Here, Education Department of both the Governments—Central and State, have not yet accepted it as an integral part of school system. It is only a few private schools in prominent cities and government schools which have employed social workers in their schools. There are no laws or legislations making social workers to work mandatorily in school system. This curbed the expansion of the scope of school social work in India. The growth achieved so far is only because of effects made by colleges of social work, associations of trained social workers, child guidance clinics and few progressive educationalists.

Social work as a profession has been introduced in our schools in the late 1950s and early 1960s. At that time the main emphasis was given on case work because social work educationalists were familiar with this type of model only. The public sector schools were the first ones where the social workers were introduced, as these schools cater largely to the middle class and the elite which were suitable as well as receptive for hosting this experiment. And the most important factor for introduction of the school social work programme in India was the placement of students (social work) for their field works in the school setting. These students sensitized the importance of school social worker through their work which led to the appointment of social workers in many cases. These placements of school social workers were undertaken for varied reasons and through various avenues.

In India, social work education was borrowed from the West. So, educational institutions of social work paid more emphasis on methods like case work and group work. However, social work educators encountered the challenge of locating field work agencies where these primary methods of social work could have been practiced. There was indeed the shortage of such field work agencies. Institutions such as Nirmala Niketan (N.N.), Tata Institute of Social Sciences (TISS) and Delhi School of Social Work (DSSW) found solution to this by establishing their own agencies.[5] But the same thing was not possible for other majority of educational institutions of social work. Therefore, they started searching large number of agencies to accommodate more and more students. Their search led them to schools. And it was felt that both the methods case work and group work can easily be practiced with the children as they are having various emotional behavioural and academic problems. In the year 1958, for the same reason Kashi Vidyapeeth, Varanasi (later known as Faculty of Social Work) also started student placements in school setting. Initially, they placed two girls in a progressive private school, namely Besant Theosophical School, under the supervision of a faculty member (Goyal, 1980). Although, this was an important breakthrough in the history of school social working in India, but, it could not be able to lead to any employment of social workers in this or any other school of Varanasi.

In 1959, Bombay initiated the placement of students with different motto; here the motto was to explore the new fields of social work through placing students to the schools. Both the colleges of social work in Bombay—Nirmala Niketan (N.N.) and Tata Institute of Social Sciences (TISS), made various efforts to "provoke and orient principals of local schools to give their services as a trial on students in fieldwork basis" and after successful demonstration persuaded them to employ social workers in their schools (D'Souza, 1965).

As the field was new so everything was taken care of and selected only those schools for student's placements, whose principal showed receptivity for the programme and were in contact with the faculty members of colleges of social work. As a result placement of student of Nirmala Niketan, Bombay in Antonio D'Souza High School, Bombay led to the appointment of social worker in the school (Desai, 1982). This paved the way for the appointment of social workers in other private schools.

The child guidance clinic of Tata Institute of Social Sciences, Bombay also did a remarkable work in the students' placement in 1960 as a part of celebration of "World Mental Health Year" (Banerjee, 1965). The clinic decided for student placement to prevent mental ill-health in the schools and did successful demonstration with the close supervision of psychiatric social worker in the clinic and the faculty in charge of Tata Institute of Social Sciences (TISS). As a result of this the school employed its own social workers in 1965, but the support remains continued by the clinic (C.G.C. Annual Report, 1960-65).

From Bombay, the idea of school social work got spread to Pune and there the local college of social work, namely Karve Institute of Social Sciences persuaded Pune Palak Shikshak Sangh (PPSS), the Pune branch of Maharashtra Parent-Teacher Association, to accept students for the placement in their private affiliate local schools. The PPSS which came into being in 1960 undertook a number of programmes for the children of its member schools other than working for Parent-teacher cooperation. It accepted student's placement in its private affiliated local schools and the successful demonstration initiated in 1964, led to the employment of social worker in local schools with persuasion by College of Social Work, namely Karve Institute of Social Sciences (KISS) under PPSS.

This was the remarkable thing happened as it was for the first time that a Parent-teacher body whose member (non-social workers) had realized the importance of having social workers in schools and this idea was also introduced in Varanasi, India. In 1964 a few private schools in Bombay also employed their own social worker even without trial. This brought into a small assistance of small group of school social workers.

The appointment of these social workers helped in making the subject of school social work recognized at the national level. Discussions were held on the theme of school social work and college social work in the Indian Conference of Social Work at its XIII Session held at Varanasi in December 1964 and these deliberations brought together a couple of school social work practitioners at a common forum. The paper presented by the workers there explored their work clearly about the case work services. The panel of experts, social work educators and other school social workers laid down a few recommendations to propagate this emerging field. The prominent among them were as follows:

(i) "Now, that the usefulness of school social work has been demonstrated and accepted in places like Bombay, we recommend that in various states the Department of Education should establish school social work sections in the Board of Education to promote social work services in schools and appoint school counsellors in the schools. The Indian Conference of Social Work and the Indian Association of Trained Social Workers should take-up this matter with the Education Commission at the Centre and the All India Teachers' Association."

(ii) "A professional social worker with experience in education setting should be appointed in the Department of Education to help in policy-making and execution."

(iii) "An introduction course in social work in the educational setting should be taught in teachers' training colleges in the country to orient teachers."

(iv) "The salary of social worker in the education setting should commensurate with his/her professional qualification and experience."

(v) "Allocation for the programme of social work should be included in the Fourth Five Year Plan and should provide for rural as well as urban areas."

But these recommendations could not be materialized and the situation remained same. The next move to introduce school social work programme was made by the Indian Association of Trained Social Workers (IATSWs) in the private schools of the Capital. IATSW undertook demonstration projects in the schools. Logically, the association would have undertaken this project in a government school, but that would be a long and difficult process which requires lots of administrative challenges and for which association was not prepared to deal with. So, the association demonstrated the project in one of the prestigious private school of Delhi in 1969 with the collaboration of Delhi School of Social Work Society.[6]

Here, the pattern adopted by the association was different from that of Bombay. The schools were made aware of the school social work programme by the trained social worker and not by the placements of students.

This demonstration was done in Saint Thomas School, as its principal was the member of the managing committee of Delhi School of Social Work (DSSW). Initially, Rupees five hundred was paid as a monthly salary to the school social worker. Out of which 2/3rd amount came from IATSW and Delhi School of Social Work Society (who sponsored the programme) and 1/3rd amount came from the Parent Teacher Association of the school. And it was negotiated that if the programme became successful in the initial two years than the whole amount of salary would be borne by the school only.[7]

To keep an eye on the programme they formed an "Implementation Committee", members of which were the members from sponsoring agencies (IATSW and DSSW Society), the principal and the school social worker hosting the project work. They all met after regular intervals of time and discussed the progress of the project, and found out solutions of the problems coming in their way.

After the two years successful demonstration of school social work services in Saint Thomas School, the management took all the responsibility of the project in 1971. Implementation Committee continues in popularizing the school social work service by sponsoring (50% subsidy for a period of one year demonstration to the new schools), guiding and arranging seminars and initiating the programme in other schools. This popularized school social work programme in Delhi, but the approach continued to predominately focus on case work and clinical approach. Although later on the workers started taking-up roles like organizing camps, Parent-teacher meeting, adopting nearby communication etc.

By now, the service was also introduced in private schools of Bombay and Pune, but Government or Municipal schools could not adopt the programme. The credit of introducing this service in Municipal schools of Bombay goes to the College of Social Work, Nirmala Niketan.

Although the service of school social work was initiated in large number of private schools of Bombay, but discontinued either because of change of Principal or Worker. As a result of which stable indigenous model of school social work is missing. So, realizing the importance of school social work and providing the stability to the field of social work education, Nirmala Niketan chose urban slums for their work. The Municipal Corporation of Bombay caters the children from these urban slums. And the problem like poverty, family breakdown, unhygienic conditions, dropouts were prevailing there. It visualized that the best way to bring a breakthrough in the plight of slum children was to provide integrated services, through the delivery of school social work services in Municipal Corporation of Bombay and placed two students in the Municipal Corporation of Greater Bombay, which resulted in the appointment of the trained social workers in the years 1971 and 1973. After that a crucial partnership between the Municipal Corporation of Greater Bombay and the college was evolved, the programme got another boost in year 1979, the International Year of the Child. Because of which the programme was extended to 15 more locations of corporation, till today this remains the biggest project. While the College of Social Work, Nirmala Niketan was busy in developing school social work in Government and Municipal Schools. The New Delhi Municipal Council (NDMC) was also contemplating to initiate such programme in their schools. At this time schools of NDMC were also facing the problem of high dropout. The education officer of this civic body had attended Seminars on School Social Work and some meeting of the Implementing Committee, so he was aware of the service. On realizing the importance of the service for reducing dropout rates and universalisation of education, and due to sound financial position of NDMC, he took initiative to introduce programme in NDMC schools. In 1985 NDMC sanctioned 15 posts of school social workers to work for its schools. But due to absence of social work supervisors, the social workers were left entirely under the charge of educationalists (those lacks social work knowledge) of NDMC and could not grow to its full shape (Gandhi, 1990).

The above mentioned experiences are the milestone in the development of school social work programme in India.

Models of School Social Work

Based on the type of school and the programme of school social work followed by the schools, Gandhi (1990) gave following four models of school social work.

School Social Work in Private Schools

Private School Independent Model

Here, the private schools run the school social work programme independently. In this model school appoints one or more than one social worker (according to their requirements) in their school. There they are provided with various facilities like separate room, allowance for home visits, clerical facilities. They work under the principal. They all are either highly qualified or have basic knowledge in the field of social work. This model aims to enable pupils to be more productive and enabled so as to make optimum use of school experience and be conscientize citizens.

(1) Focus of the Model

In this model the prime focus is on the individual. Individual's problem is considered as top priority. In this the social worker deals with the problems like emotional disturbance, learning problems, parent-child and teacher-child relationships, high expectation of parents from child etc. For this, either parents of the child, teachers, or principal refers the child having problems or sometimes, students themselves approach the social worker with problems they are facing. The social worker is expected to be well-equipped to deal with wide range of problems students encounter in the school setting. School social worker networks and collaborates with stakeholders like teachers, peers, family members, neighbour, and the community to resolve the problems. Social worker makes home visits, whenever required.

Sometimes, for handling the cases social workers also undertake the advice of experts like speech therapist, psychologist, psychiatrist, special educator etc., depending upon the requirement.

The availability of school social work within the school not only helps the child, but also carries out tasks effectively and enriches the educational inputs of the school. School social workers deal with problems and challenges faced by children in the school, they also work at preventive-level. Many schools entrust their social workers with the responsibilities of undertaking preventive programmes under various names like—life-skill education programmes, growing-up seminars and such others, where information is provided to children on diverse issues that they may encounter such as drug addiction, peer pressure, sex-education, especially to children in puberty stage so that their adolescence is not a turbulent stage. Providing career counselling is yet another area where social workers play critical role.

The tasks performed by school social workers, according to this model, may be categorized into five broad areas as follows:

1. Helping Children having Problems.
2. Educational Enrichment Programmes.
3. Parents and Teacher-related tasks.
4. Administrative Work.
5. Non-social Work Tasks.

One of the important area of tasks of school social workers is their engagement in Socially Useful and Productive Work (SUPW) introduced in school curriculum. Wide range of activities is included under the SUPW, which differs from school to school. The primary objective of SUPW is to make the school children encounter with the social realities. SUPW has two salient components—production-oriented work which means acquisition of skills and production of tangible and consumable goods. For instance, some schools have units for recycling of waste materials and the children work there. They learn to conserve environment. Certain schools have handicraft units, participation in which makes the pupils learn value of human labour and dignity of labour. And the other one is service-oriented work which benefits the community and develops a sense of awareness and commitment among pupils. Here, children go to nearby slum community and undertake programmes, like "each-one-teach-one" or adopt a grandparent, and similar others. Children are exposed to harsh realities like poverty, discrimination, child labour, destitution and they learn to bring some positive change in the situation of disadvantaged groups, through their work.

The social worker takes charge of both types of services under SUPW. Generally, the principal, some senior teachers and school social worker together form an implementation committee for SUPW, in which social worker coordinates the programme and looks after its day-to-day implementation while teachers supports him/her in the work.

The school social workers working with SUPW are found to be performing number of tasks which are as follows:

- planning of SUPW activities;
- organizing and implementation orientation of students and teachers;
- liaison with the teachers and supervising them;
- evaluating students;
- maintaining records;
- coordinating and executing various SUPW activities;
- evaluating and reviewing the programme; and
- coordinating teachers and parents regarding SUPW activities.

This apart, private schools also conduct integrated education programme for slow learners or partially deaf children so that a facilitative environment can be provided to these children and they can be included in the mainstream education. Social workers carry out following tasks under the gamut of "inclusive education":

- undertaking case history of the child;
- maintain records;
- arranging experts for periodic medical and non-medical evaluation of special need children;
- organising the conference to monitor the progress of a particular case;
- case work service to the special need child in order to solve their problems;
- counselling the parents of children with special needs as well as other children;
- counselling the 'normal' children to facilitate integration of the children with special needs;
- liaison with outside agencies to procure employment for children with special needs;
- liaison with grant giving agencies;
- liaison with volunteers and voluntary agencies to help these children; and
- teaching the slow learners.

It may be noted that within the model of "School Social Work in Private Schools", a high level of variability is observed in terms of activities taken-up. For instance, in place of inclusive education programme for children with physical and/or mental disabilities, some schools may have programmes for economically poor, but gifted children, and social workers organize seminars for vocational guidance special training programmes etc. For all these programme related experts are invited.

In this private school independent model, social workers have enough time and opportunities along with greater flexibility of taking-up activities that suit their school's vision and programmatic intricacies. However, certain disadvantages too may be examined with the model. As being the part of school system, sometimes social workers are not able to carve out their own role-identity and may have to adhere to the tasks provided by school authorities, which, at times, may include taking substitution classes.

Private School Collaborative Model

In this model, private schools run the school social work programme in collaboration with other agencies like child-guidance clinic or Parents-Teacher Association.

FOCUS—The focus of this model is to help out students, having social and emotional difficulties, with the collaboration of various agencies like child guidance clinics and Parent-Teacher Association (PTA). In this the programme is so planned that it benefits both the school and the collaborating agency. Such a programme fulfils logical means of objectives. Certain factors that increase the desirability of this collaborative model may be delineated.

Many times, school social workers are ill-equipped to deal with social and psychological problems faced by students. Such tough cases can be referred to child guidance clinics where specialized services may be procured for the affected child. School related problems like indiscipline, adjustment problems, school phobia, etc., are the major referrals to the child guidance clinic.

This model provides enough scope to the mental health workers to detect, assess and to intervene in the child's problem as the child remains in the school for longer hours.

It also provides ample opportunity to approach concerned parents and get their support as they generally are more willing to co-operate, with school than with clinic.

The school social workers perform variety of tasks falling in the realm of both curative as well as preventive approaches. These tasks include case work services, counselling of parents and teachers, home visits, family life education, and group counselling etc.

Certain benefits of this collaborative model may be spelled out. As this model is based on the collaboration between school and certain agency working for child-well-being, so the schools could get the benefits of other professionals, along with social workers with nominal charges. In addition, the collaborating agency such as child guidance clinic is also able to expand the scope of its services, which otherwise, in Indian context, is not so popular. The parents who are having children with problems may not directly approach the child guidance clinic, but its association with school bridges the gaps.

On the flip side, there are certain disadvantages with this model. The school social worker being the part-time staff in the school may not be able to develop rapport with students and teachers and may not be able to carry out range of activities as his/her counterpart in the school with independent model.

School Social Work in Municipal Schools

Municipal School Independent Model

In this model, the education system of the Municipality runs the school social work programme independently. This model is practiced by Education Department of New Delhi Municipal Council (NDMC). In this model of school social work, the focus is on the community children, especially the economically deprived ones, who need to avail the services of school system. The goal of this model is to attain universalisation of elementary education and to minimize the high dropout rate of children in its school. The target is primarily the group of those children who are facing problem of exclusion from the school or absenteeism.

Social workers intervene with children who are facing problems in adjustment in the school, primarily because of being poor and deprived. Most of these children are first generation learners. Largely, their parents do not understand the importance of education. Children either have to engage in household chores and taking care of siblings as their parents go out to earn or these children themselves earn. Schools, too, are not attractive enough. Quality education is a big challenge. Hence, most children do not continue and drop out of the school. School social workers network with families and schools so as to make the education environment of the school conducive for the deprived children.

A manual, on the roles and responsibilities of school social worker in NDMC schools, was developed with the joint effort of NDMC and the members of the Indian Association of Trained Social Workers. According to the manual, school social workers have to discharge their duties in the following three capacities—

(a) As Field Worker

- He or she has to carry out surveys in assigned areas to identify out of school children (of school going age but not attending schools) and help them in their enrolment.
- Identifying and contacting agencies for psychological, psychiatric and other types of professional help.
- Conduct group work with children.
- Maintain good rapport with staff members and work for staff development.
- Develop and maintain rapport with community people and practice community organization.
- Help execution of non-formal education and adult education programme.
- Run summer schools.
- Organize volunteer services, if required.

(b) As Case Worker/Counsellor

- He or she undertakes various cases of children needing help and counsel them to solve their problem.
- Counsels parents and teachers in order to help out children from problem.

(c) As Office Worker

- He or she maintains a list of various agencies which are useful for referrals.
- Maintains records of whatever work they did with children and periodic surveys they conducted in the community.
- Maintains records about the meetings held with the senior teachers, Parent-Teacher Association (PTA) etc.

This apart, the manual also specifies that each worker had to cater four neighbouring schools of a particular area. But all records, salary, leave, attendance etc., of social workers are kept with the headmaster of one of these four schools and that school is called the parent school.

(d) Facilities Provided

Separate room for counselling services furnished with light, fan, sitting arrangements, toys for children and almirah for record keeping.

Social workers have to spend seven hours per day, in which five hours are assigned for school hours and rest two hours for community services. The community timings are not fixed and social worker can meet the community people, especially parents of out of school children according to their availability.

(e) Conceptual Base

In this model the social worker needs to have knowledge about the sociological and psychological factors that act as barriers to provision of right to education to all the children at least up to 14 years of age. They are expected to play role of mediators and advocates to realize the right to education.

But this model has somewhat failed to take its full shape due to various reasons, few of them are mentioned below :

- No effective support system was developed to provide facilities to the pupil.
- For this, allied services and professional help other than social workers were required which they could not get.
- The model was supervised by educationalists, who did not realize the importance of the skills of social workers.
- The members of school management, teachers and principals were not properly oriented with the scope and strengths of social work discipline in the school setting.
- This model falls close to the model given by Costin's "School Community Pupil Model".

Municipal School Collaborative Model

In this model, the education system of the Municipal Corporation runs the school social work programme in collaboration with other agency such as Child Guidance Clinic.

In this model the focus is on the deprived and disadvantaged children of slum who do not have resources to fulfil, their basic needs. So, the focus of this model is to provide package in the field of education, health, recreation and promotion of home, school and community relation.

The goal of this model is to develop school community programme in order to give assistance to the deprived and disadvantaged children and alleviate conditions which affect child's learning and social functioning.

The target groups of this model are school, family, and community nearby school.

Poverty, deprivation and disadvantage are the factors having adverse effects on child development. The tasks performed by social workers are based on the identification of hurdles that affect learning of a child, to develop community understanding and support of the school, to develop school community programme, to assist disadvantage children so that they can make maximum use of school service. The social worker has the knowledge of school and community factors that act as barriers in effective school education for the out of school children and he/she also has expertise to nullify such barriers to ensure right to education to all the children.

This model is closer to the model given by Alder, that is "Community School Model". This apart, this model also has some of the characteristics of "School Change Model".

School Social Work in Kerala

Kerala has the highest rate of suicide as compared to any other state of India. Its reported rate is 30.6 per 1 lakh population. Which is three times higher than the national average.

A study on Prevalence of Stress among school children in Kerala (Dinesh, 2011) was done to understand the prevalence of stress-level in school children of Kerala. The results indicated that more than 90 per cent of the school children of Kerala are facing more than normal-level of stress and tension either in their family or in their school.

Suresh Kumar (n.d.) emphasizes on the importance of developing locally and culturally relevant and feasible strategies to implement for preventing suicide attempts. He also talked about school-based interventions which includes life skill education, counselling programmes, teacher's training, and liaison with Mental Health Services.

Conclusion

School social work has a great potential to bring the needed change in the education system as well as facilitating a conducive teaching-learning environment. In the present chapter importance of social workers in the school setting was discussed. History of emergence of school social work in various countries, like United States of America (USA), England and India was delineated. The chapter also discusses various models of school social work that are functional in the country and abroad. It depicts the inter-linkage between pupil's school system and the community. The chapter gives details of the context in which social work is practiced and can be established. The next chapter provides the scholarship on literature on school social work and methodological underpinnings of present study.

Notes

1. The survey was conducted on 50 State Departments of Education and District of Columbia and Puerto Rico.
2. In contrast to U.S.A. and India, the school social work in England is known as "Education Social Work". However, for the sake of uniformity the term "school social work" *in lieu* of "Education Social Work" will be used in this text.
3. The Social Service departments came into existence in 1971 following the recommendation of Seebohm Committee. They provide comprehensive service in a defined area, in the field of health, welfare, nursing, and education to persons and families in need through the trained social workers.
4. The description of tasks undertaken by Social Service Department in connection with Social Children is based on the Welfare of London Children, Inner London Education Authority (1973) (Mimeographed).
5. This is not to suggest that the placement of students was the only reason for the establishment of these agencies.

6. Delhi School of Social Work Society was a voluntary body which used to run College of Social Work—the Delhi School of Social Work, before it started receiving grants from University Grants Commission.
7. This and the following two paragraphs are based on the records of the Implementation Committee for School Social Work Project, under the auspices of Indian Association of Trained Social Workers, Delhi Branch (1969-1974).

References

Appelbaum and Chambliss (1997), Cited in Article, "Power and Conformity in Today's Schools", Justin Saldana, Ph.D., published in *International Journal of Humanities and Social Science*, Vol. 3, No. 1; January 2013.

Banerjee, G.R. (1965), "School Social Services: Its Potentialities", *The Indian Journal of Social Work*, Vol. 26, No. 3.

Child Guidance Clinic, B.J. Wadia Hospital for Children, *Annual Reports*, 1960-1965 (Mimeographed).

Costin, L.B. (1978), *Social Work Services in School: Historical Perspective and Current Directions*, Continuing Education Series #8, Washington, D.C.: National Association of Social Works.

Counts, George S. (1932), *Dare the School Build a New Social Order?* Carbondale, IL: Southern Illinois University Press.

D'Souza, C., Syed. R., Sonaya, S. (1965), *Social Work Forum*, Vol. 3, No. 2.

Denaull, L. (1978 b), *"Title T of E SEA: Utilizing the Social Work Service"* in Federal Legislation and the School Social Worker, Washington, D.C.: National Association of Social Workers.

Desai, A. (1982), Then the Principal of Nirmala Niketan, *Personal Interview*, June.

Dinesh, S. (2011), *Prevalence of stress among school children in Kerala*, International Society for Analytical and Molecular Morphology. Retrieved on June 28, 2011 from http://www.isamm.org/prevalence-of-stress-among-school-children-in-kerala.htm

Fredricksen, H. (1948), *The Child and His Welfare*, California: W.H. Freeman & Company, University of California.

Friedlander, W.A. (1963), *Introduction to Social Welfare*, New Delhi: Prentice Hall of India Pvt. Ltd.

G.A. Russell (1994), "The Impact of the Philosophus Autodidactus: Pocockes, John Locke and the Society of Friends", in: G.A. Russell (ed.), *The 'Arabick' Interest of the Natural Philosophers in Seventeenth Century,* England: Brill Publishers.

Gandhi, A. (1990), *School Social Work,* New Delhi: Commonwealth Publishers.

Goyal, C.P. (1980), "A Resume of the Development of School Social Work Movement in Kashi Vidyapeeth" (Unpublished Paper).

Henslin (1999), Cited in Article, "Power and Conformity in Today's Schools", Justin Saldana, Ph.D., published in *International Journal of Humanities and Social Science,* Vol. 3, No. 1, January 2013.

Joshi, S. (1996), *Child Survival, Health and Social Work Intervention,* New Delhi: Concept Publishing Company.

MacMillan, K. (1980), The Education Welfare Officer: Past, Present, and Future, *Linking Home and School,* M. Craft, J. Raynor and L. Cohen, London: Harper & Row.

Mintzies, P.M. (1978), *The Emergency School Aid Act: Implications for Social Work Practices,* Washington D.C.: National Association of Social Workers.

Panda, A.K. (2005), *Elderly Women in Mega Polish,* New Delhi: Concept Publishing Company.

Plowden Report (1967), *Children and Their Primary Schools,* London: HMSO.

Robinson, M. (1978), *School and Social Work,* London: Routledge and Kegan Paul.

Saldana, Justin (2013), "Power and Conformity in Today's Schools", *International Journal of Humanities and Social Sciences.* Vol. 3, No. 1.

Seebohm Report (1968), *Report of the Committee on Local Authority and Allied Personal Social Services,* London: HMSO.

Sikkema, M. (1951), "School Social Work Services", *Social Work Year Book,* Margaret, E.H., (Ed.), New York: American Association of Social Workers.

Stuart, M. (1970), *"One Hundred Years of London Education"*; 1870-1970, Allen Lane, London: The Penguin Press.

Suresh Kumar, P.N. (2004), "Current Research in Suicide in India", *IMA Academy of Medical Specialties, Kerala State Chapter,* Retrieved on June 25, 2011, from http://www.manasikarogyam.com/index.php/files/category/6-english-books?download=Asuicide-prevention-manual-for-primary-care-givers&usg=AFQjCNF78LZcpsG3zG8-XRFJFUG CNARb8w

Suresh Kumar, P.N. (2004), "An Analysis of Suicide Attempters *versus* Completers in Kerala", *Indian Journal of Psychiatry,* 46(2).

The Education Act, 1944 (1944), London: HMSO.

Usaj, K., Shine, J.K., Mandlawitz, M. (2009), Response to Intervention: New Roles for School Social Workers, *School Social Work Association of America,* Retrieved on August 19, 2009, from http://www.wiscons inpbisnetwork.org/assets/files/2012%20 Conference/Session%20 Material/Roles_School_Social_Workers_ RTI.pdf

Weatherly, R. (1978), *The Education for all Handicapped Children Act of 1975*, Washington, D.C.: National Association of Social Workers.

2
Review of Literature and Research Methodology

School is one of the important units in developing child's personality. However, not all the children are able to avail the facilities and inputs provided in the school equally and some children require additional support. The reasons may be varied and lie in social, cultural, economic, educational or environmental unfavourable conditions. It has been demonstrated that by suitable interventions one can help children to overcome the disadvantage conditions. Such interventions generally come in the purview of social work in school setting. Below is the review of literature available on the effectiveness of school social work and its dimensions.

A thematic review is done below with twin objectives—one, challenges in the education system, which, in turn, reflect the scope of school social work in the Indian setting and two, existing status of school social workers, the roles played by them and the impediments encountered.

Review of Literature

Educational Scenario in India

Battle and Lewis (2002) identify the significance of education in today's world. They state that in this era of globalization and technological revolution, education plays a vital role in the development of human capital and is linked with an individual's well-being and opportunities for better living. In the same wavelength, Sexton (2000) brings out that education ensures the acquisition of knowledge and skills that enable individuals to increase their productivity and improve their quality of life. This increase in productivity also leads towards new sources of earning which enhances the economic growth of a country.

There have been many studies done to examine the factors that influence students' performance. Crosnoe, Johnson and Elder (2004) categorize these factors as student factors (personal motivation, aspirations, personality types, adjustment abilities etc.); family factors (socio-economic condition, parental educational levels, family culture in relation to education etc.); school factors (teachers' attitudes, infrastructure, management, and such others); and peer factors (peer pressure, bullying, acceptance in group, and so on). Besides other factors, socio-economic status is one of the most researched and debated variable that contribute towards the academic performance of students. Adams (1996) finds that the socio-economic status of learners affects the quality of their academic performance. The researcher cites the reason as the low socio-economic status has negative effect on the academic performance of students because the basic needs of students remain unfulfilled and hence they do not perform better academically. Adeyinka (2009) too confirms the findings of the above study with his research work that maladaptive behaviour arise when parents lack responsibility of their parenthood and that children from economically disadvantaged background are more likely to have poor academic performance because they lack some basic amenities such as food, clothing and shelter.

Further, Roberts (2007) examines the theory of Educational Productivity propounded by Walberg (1981) that determined three groups of nine factors based on effective, cognitive and behavioural skills for optimization of learning that affect the quality of academic performance. Aptitude includes ability, development and motivation; instruction covers amount and quality; and environment contains home, classroom, peers and television. Another interesting aspect illustrated by many research findings is that the academic performance of students heavily depends upon the parental involvement in their academic activities to attain the higher level of quality in academic success (Barnard, 2004; Henderson, 1988; Shumox & Lomax, 2001).

Hussain (2006) studies 'guidance' as a factor in academic performance. Students often face a lot of problems in developing positive study attitudes and study habits. He demonstrates that guidance is of the factor through which a student can improve his/her study attitudes and study habits and is directly proportional to academic achievement. Children who are properly guided by their parents perform well in the examinations. Guidance from teachers also affects the performance of students.

Let us now look at the challenges from the teachers' side. Bolusteve and Sanni (2013) maintain that in order to identify hidden talents among their pupils, teachers themselves should be multi-talented and sensitive enough to recognize talents among children. They claim that, unfortunately, Indian teachers frequently do not focus on this and are more concerned about their subject knowledge. International schools expect their teachers to help students in drama, debate, dance, music, art and craft and many other activities. It is not possible to develop well rounded students if teachers are not well rounded themselves.

Likewise, Bhatnagar (2012) laments that newspapers are full of news items of corporal punishment, physical abuse and sexual exploitation, kidnap, rape by the teacher perpetrator on children-victims, thereby blotting the image of Indian teachers in the international arena. He questions the credibility and character of such teachers in the Indian society that has traditionally given utmost respect to the teachers equating them with the God. Teachers' arrogance, perpetration and uncalled for behaviours drift the students away from the school system. Due to these factors, school is not a place of attraction for children.

The research studies reviewed above shows that school systems are of prime importance in the social development and national development. Academic performance of a child in the school is dependent on many factors other than his/her hard work and motivation. These factors are—socio-economic status, parental guidance and encouragement, learning environment at school and home and such others. Teachers' mental health also plays crucial role in students' learning and overall education process. Peck and

Mitchell (1962) discuss the poor mental health in teacher. They suggested that a maladjusted teacher who is suffering from anxiety or personal problem cannot avoid communicating his insecurity to his students.

The White House Conference Preliminary Reports (1930)—"Mental Health may be defined as the adjustment of individuals to themselves and the world at large with a maximum of effectiveness, satisfactions, cheerfulness, and socially considerate behaviour and the ability of facing and accepting the realities of life."

Today in this complex world where nobody have time for them also and everybody is moving or racing for this materialistic life. Therefore, the mental health is a growing concern for all people especially for young ones and old people, because both need others to support and if they do not get positive response their mental health starts decline.

The New Educational Policy (1986) as well as National Mental Health Policy (1982) stressed on the need for promotion and prevention of mental health and related problems. Childhood is the most vulnerable period in the entire lifespan of man. In the initial period of childhood or early childhood, family is the very convenient place for promoting child's mental health. But at school child spends half of his day in school and rest with the family and friends. At this age they are highly dependent on their environment (school, home, friend circle) so their mental promotion also depends on both the child and the stress on support system presents in his family, school and community (Dr. Marry Venus Joseph—*Mental Health in Classroom*).

According to Institute of Medicine, 1989 almost 3 per cent of school age children suffers from serious mental illness such as psychosis, depression, suicide thought, serious attention problems, or obsessive-compulsive disorders. So, for the development of a child it is very much important to identify the child having psychological problems at early stage of life and then target them for intervention. Otherwise these psycho-social problems are turned school dropouts, drug and alcohol abuse, juvenile delinquency etc. Children who are not doing well in school may suffer from these kinds of psycho-social problems and are unlikely to perform well in school in later life.

Division of Mental Health, WHO, 1994 gave a model framework for school mental health programmes.

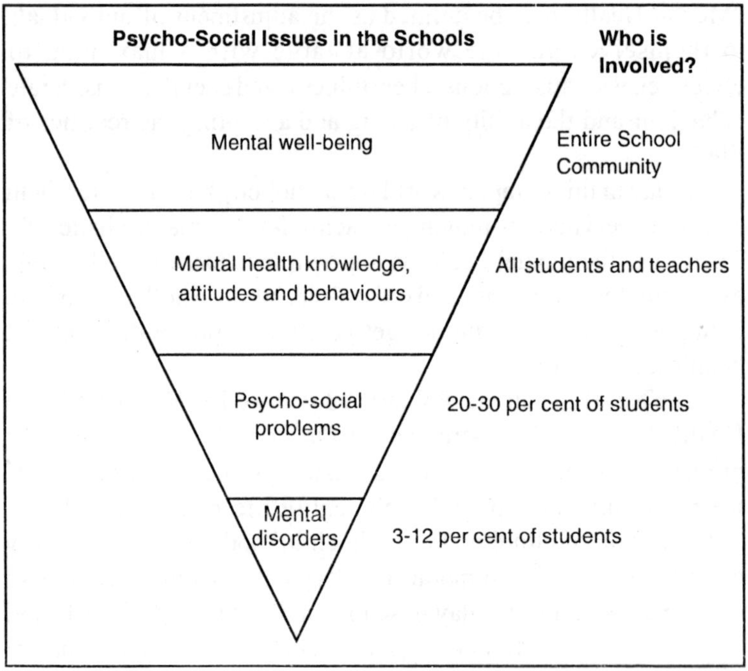

Figure 2.1: A Model Framework for School Mental Health Programmes

Figure 2.1 explains the psycho-social and mental health issues present in the schools and also indicates who is likely to be affected by issues, like issues of men well-being and psycho-social competence will affect the entire school (students, teachers, administrators etc.). So, there is need for specific mental health programmes which may address these issues and create a healthy school community.

Mental health knowledge, attitudes, and behaviour affect all students and teachers. So, interventions may be useful for identification and handling of psycho-social and mental health problems.

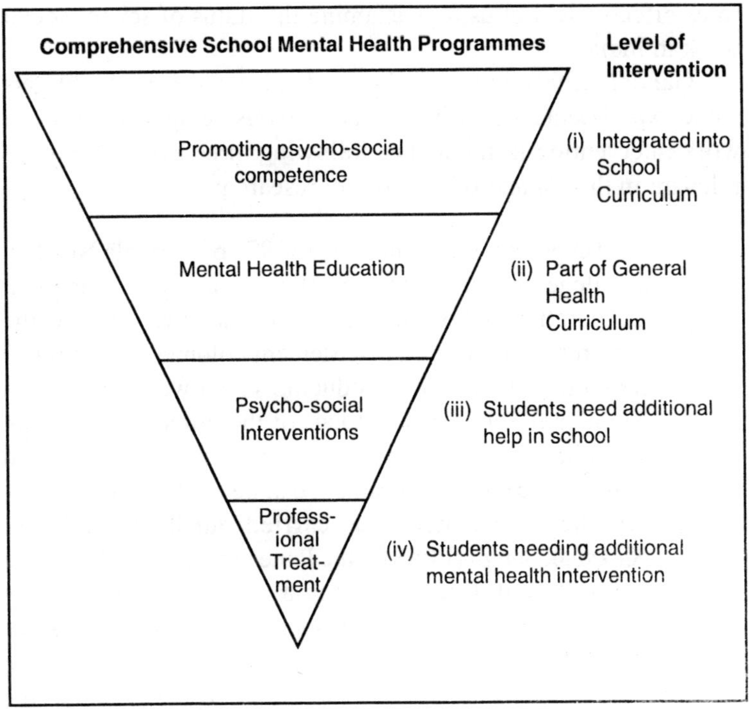

Figure 2.2: Intervention Model

WHO has also given an intervention model (division of mental health, WHO, 1994).

For the effectiveness of the programme all the four levels are needed, but the focus is generally seen up to only one or two levels at first. However, the importance of school has also been recognized increasingly by the policy-makers and school education is considered as a means for national and social development in developing countries. So, this intervention model seems helpful for achieving the desired goal.

The review of literature, beyond doubt illustrates the vast scope of social workers in the education setting. They need to work with students, their parents and other family members and school authorities and teachers. Though teachers are the backbone of school system, social workers can play no less important role in facilitating all the actors (student, school and family) perform their roles effectively. Let us now examine the status of school social work in India.

Gandhi (1990), in her book on school social work highlights some experiments indicating various models being used as social work intervention in India. The following three experiments are relevant in the context of the present research:

1. First experiment was initiated in 1971 by Nirmala Niketan, a college of social work, in collaboration with Municipal Corporation School of Greater Bombay catering to the children of slums and resettlement colonies. The college took the initiative of introducing social work services in Municipal Schools. The focus of the programme was on providing home, school, and community relationship so that the learning environment can be made conducive.
2. Another experiment was carried out by Pune Palak Shikshak Sangh (PPSS)—the Pune branch of Maharashtra State Parent-Teacher Association has been actively associated with the school of social work programme since 1960. Here, the Parent body was rigorously involved in the school programme for the overall development of the children.
3. Like Nirmala Niketan experiment, New Delhi Municipal Council (NDMC) in Delhi initiated social work services in 1985 to attain universalisation of elementary education and to check the high dropout rates prevalent in the schools. Before employing school social worker, the education department of NDMC noted that 14 per cent of the children of the age group of 6-11 years residing in its area were not attending school and further the dropout rate prevalent in its school at primary level was as high as 45 per cent. After the induction of professional social workers, designated as student welfare workers in the NDMC schools, the percentage of children not attending school fell from 14 per cent in 1964 to 1.5 per cent 1978-79 and dropout rate which in as high as 45 per cent in 1964 reduced to 2 per cent in 1979. Looking at the above data one cannot deny the contribution of professional social workers both

towards the achievement of universalization of elementary education and in reduction of dropout in primary schools of New Delhi Municipal Council (NDMC).

Some research studies in India (Joshi, 1996; Aggarwal and Kapoor, 1998) also suggest that family awareness on the importance of education and parental participation in children's education contribute to better academic performance of children's in school. The school social workers indeed can play a significant role in enhancing conducive family environment for effective learning.

Bowen (1996) in her article "A Role for School Social Workers in promoting student success through School Family Partnership" highlights a social work intervention that enhanced parents' ability towards creating home conditions, which help in learning and promoting family involvement in home learning activities. The intervention was carried out by both teachers and parents with the academic and behaviour problems of the five targeted kindergarten and first grade students. The findings support other research studies indicating that parents' educational involvement promotes students' achievement.

In another study, Henderson and Berla (1994) observe that students' school performance at the beginning of the intervention was assessed by teachers' qualitative descriptions of academic social behaviour. Parents' perceptions of performance were also documented before the intervention began. The assessment of students' performance during and at the end of the intervention was based on the perception of teachers and parents. Parents and teachers perceived a variety of favourable results because of the social work intervention. Most significant of these results were improvement in students' academic and social behaviours and improved Parent-teacher communication. Other notable positive effects of interventions included more positive teacher's perceptions of student's future progress and parents' increased knowledge of their children's learning styles and need, greater self-esteem among students and greater parental satisfaction with school.

Result of the intervention suggests that school social workers can promote student and school success by directly facilitating school-family communications and ensuring that educational resources are shared with parents. The small sample size and lack of experimental group makes it difficult to generalize the findings to a larger social context.

Reddy (1995) has conducted a qualitative research to access the performance of dropout children with ecological perspective so as to offer a suitable plan of intervention. Findings infer that the poor economic status, unhygienic and poor living conditions, lack of awareness, negative attitudes of parents, unattractive conditions in schools, negative image of teachers as perceived by parents and children, and the poor performance of teachers, lack of interventions to motivate parents etc. are some of the factors responsible for the non-enrollment and dropouts among the disadvantaged groups. Social interventions in the form of massive awareness and counselling programmes to motivate parents, children and community were suggested. For attitudinal and pedagogical changes teacher's training programmers were recommended. Indeed, school social work has wide scope to make significant contribution in this regard.

Joshi (1996) has studied the effectiveness of social work intervention in improving the health and growth of under-five children belonging to urban slum community. To evaluate the impact of social work intervention before and after treatment, experimental and control (group) data were compared and analyzed for suitable statistical measures. The finding of the research study pointed out that social work intervention improved the health of under-five slum children as also the knowledge and attitude regarding healthcare of under-five amongst the target women.

Collaboration between social work and education is widely recognized as a valuable partnership for the social and educational needs of disadvantaged children and their families. Research studies in India and around the world suggest that parent's investment in child education is the most effective way to boost learning achievement. Following studies from West show the effectiveness of intervention in school setting with disadvantages of children and families.

A multi-dimensional study by Bronstein and Kelly (1998) highlights significance of school social workers. In the study, the social worker took the role of mediator between home and school, spending increasing time consulting teachers, and meeting family members. The most critical factor identified was the need to develop an intensive home base family outreach treatment plan.

Another research study by Bowen and Bowen (1998) had implications for school social workers intervention with individuals and groups. It examines the interplay of home environment risk factors, teacher's support and student academic performance and effective investment in schooling. The study examines student academic achievement (grades) and education investment (or perception that school participation is meaningful) as salient outcome variable that can be expected to promote the long-term desirable goal of high educational attainment. The result of the research study suggests that home and academic culture proved to be an important factor for the student achievement. After teacher's support, home had the second strongest direct effect on the educational investment. The authors claim that school social workers can target student's home and academic culture in variety of ways.

Kumar (1989) maintains that attitudes of teachers and students towards school social work programme are likely to influence effectiveness of social work practice in schools. She examines the content and mode of their functioning. Her study was based on the premise that the mere fact that the school social worker provides professional intervention does not necessarily mean that such intervention has been successful in achieving its objectives. She has stressed a need to evaluate contemporary social work practice in schools because there is not much conceptual clarity about the specific measurable objectives of school social work practice against which the professional activities of practitioners may be appraised.

Kumar suggests that the supervision inputs by school social workers in the community by services and programmes need to be re-analyzed. This would result in image building of the school social workers distinctly different from that of a teacher and school psychologist.

The review of literature done above provided an insight into the roles and effectiveness of school social work. However, a few research gaps may well be delineated. The studies are geographic and culture specific and therefore, the results may not be homogeneously applied to other settings. School social work in India is still in its nascent stage. There is high level of variability among the designation, role, position, status, authority and the support system available for social workers in the schools. In fact, schools do not exhibit uniformity even in terms of recruiting social workers. There is a need to conduct study that reflects this contextual variability in terms of social work response in various schools, with presence or absence of social workers.

Added to these studies have shown the positive impact of social work intervention in schools, but no comparison is made between the schools with social workers to those where no social workers are recruited. There is also a need to document the efforts made by schools without social workers in addressing to the psycho-social needs of the pupils or establishing lesions with parents and larger community. Further, research attention needs to be focused on the challenges faced by school social workers in performing their roles in consonance with the professional demands as well as encountering dilemmas in the same when school authorities expect some other tasks and roles from them. A study on school social work is also relevant and useful from the point of view of the social work profession for several reasons—

- The study would work in the direction of providing a logical place of school social workers in the school system. The study would also note down various experiences of social workers. This in turn provides various guidelines useful to the school social workers in directing and assessing their practice.
- Secondly, a large number of colleges, departments of social work in the country have school social work in their theory classes and fieldwork placement of student in the school. So, this requires lot of literature on school social work both for the educators and students. As social work practitioners have not written much about the difficulties and the prospects of the field in which they were

establishing themselves. So, the present study aims to document the major experiments in field of school social work.

A number of studies have been conducted in the area of school social work, but the researcher could not find any comparison between school with social work and school without social work.

In this backdrop, the objectives and methodological details of the present study may be delineated.

Research Methodology

Statement of the Problem

Education is considered as the road to empowerment. It is taken as a crucial component to facilitate human potential to expand and realize to its fullest. However, there are several shortcomings in the education system as well as challenges in linking numerous children to access and avail school education.

Even after the enactment of "Right to Education" in Indian context, it is still a far reaching dream to provide quality education to all the children of the country.

School social workers have the necessary capacity and expertise to make the education system accessible to all the children, deal with the bottlenecks to ensure quality education and address individual problems among children that hamper their educational attainments.

In this context, the present study intended to understand the roles and functions performed by social workers in school settings. At present, there is high variation in schools regarding social workers' presence, roles and functions. Certain private schools have appointed social workers while in some others 'counsellors' are there. Likewise, in Government schools, civil society organizations are performing tasks of social workers and many private as well as Government schools do not have social workers. The present study has compared the two types of schools—with social workers and without social workers. It gave vivid evidence of the roles and functions of social workers in the school setting.

Objectives of the Study

The primary objective of this research is to identify different and diverse benefits of social worker's involvement in child's learning. Emphasis has been on two major aspects—first, the study intends to discover exact roles and contributions made and challenges encountered by school social workers involved in school students' academic and social development and second is to compare the schools with social workers to those where no social workers are recruited. In connection, the following specific objectives are delineated:

- To trace the school having school social workers and document the tasks they are performing.
- To identify the schools without social workers and examine their response related to school social work related tasks.
- To look into the perception of the Head, teachers and children towards school social wo k.
- To compare the response of school with social workers and without social workers towards the mental health needs of the students.
- To appraise the differences between the school with social workers and those without it in terms of tasks involved in facilitating teaching-learning environment.
- To present an overview of the school social work service and make recommendation for its future practice.

Research Questions

Based on the objectives mentioned above, the study has the following salient research questions :

- What is the profile of schools employing school social workers and those without social workers?
- Whether social workers are providing a helping hand to develop children's personality and their relationship with their environment?
- Are social workers accepted by the school principal,

teachers and other staff as important staff member of their school system?
- What are the activities carried out by the social workers at the preventive, promotion and corrective level with the aim it brings positive changes in the personality of the students?
- How much time given per week by the social workers for non-academic activities?
- What is the role of social workers in liaison with school-home- community?

Operational Definitions

The study would use following standard terms while undertaking the research process. Operational definitions of certain important terms are as follows:

School

A school is a formal system or an institution to provide education to children. It is a division of an educational institution constituting of several grades or classes. A school is an institution meant for the teaching of students or pupils under the direction of teachers. Most countries have systems of formal education, which is commonly compulsory. In these systems, a student progress through a series of schools. The names for these schools vary by country, but generally include primary school for young children and secondary school for teenagers who have completed primary education. An institution where higher education is taught is commonly called a University College or University. For the purpose of the study, school is the institution where formal education up to 12th standard is provided.

School Social Worker

The school social worker means social worker employed in school for home-school, school-community or home-school-community liaison (including part-time or full-time, trained or untrained) irrespective of the condition whether his/her designation is school social worker or counsellor or equivalent to these.

Case Work

Social case work is the primary method of social work, based on one-to-one relationship, in which knowledge of the science of human relations, and skill in relationship are used to mobilize capacities in the individual and resources in the community appropriate for better adjustment between the client and all or any part of his total environment (Bowers, 1949).

Group Work

Social group work is method through which individuals in groups in social agency setting are helped by a worker who guides their interaction in programme activities so that they may relate themselves to others and experiences growth opportunities in accordance with their needs and capacities to the end of the individual, group and community development (Trecker, 1955).

Further, other terms used in the study would be explained as and when they are used for the first time.

Research Design

With the aim to appraise the efficacy of roles and functions performed by social workers in school setting, the present study, through comparative analysis between schools having social workers and those without social workers, adheres to descriptive research design.

Universe of the Study

All the schools of National Capital Territory of Delhi comprise the Universe of the Study.

Sampling Process and Method

As the research was based on Delhi schools so the researcher first divided Delhi into four zones—East, West, North and South. Then

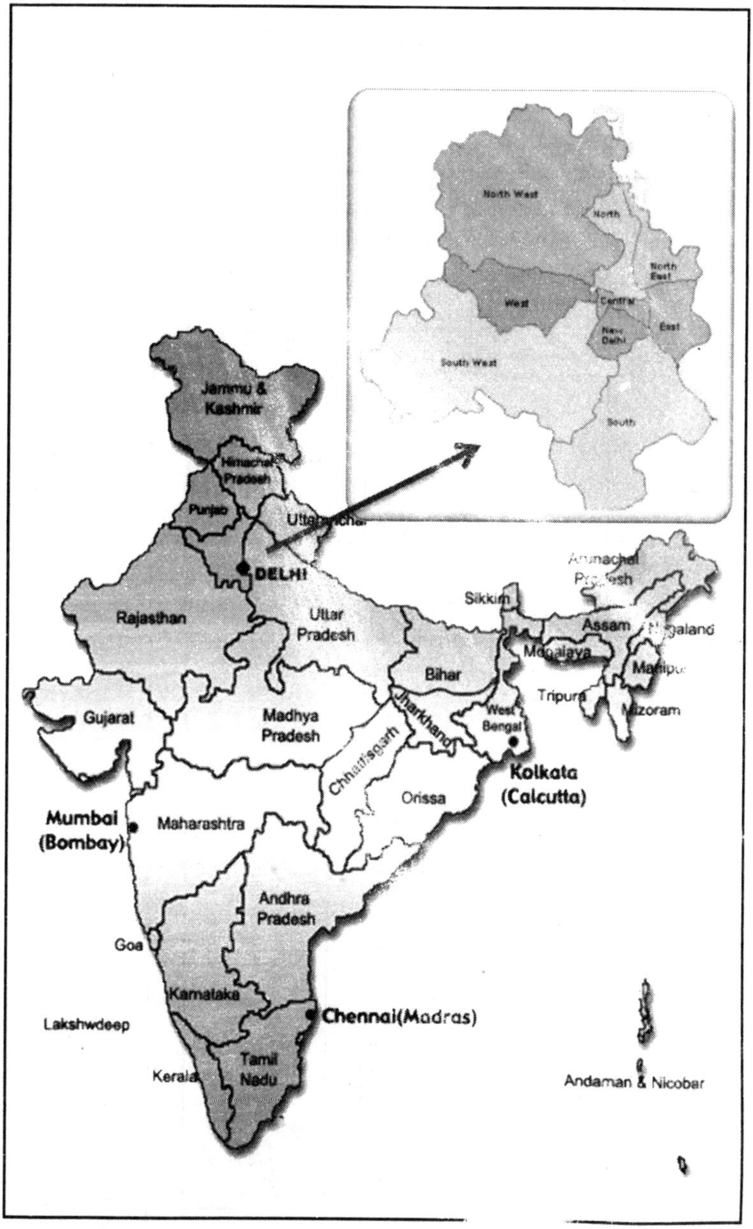

Figure 2.3: Map of India Showing Delhi

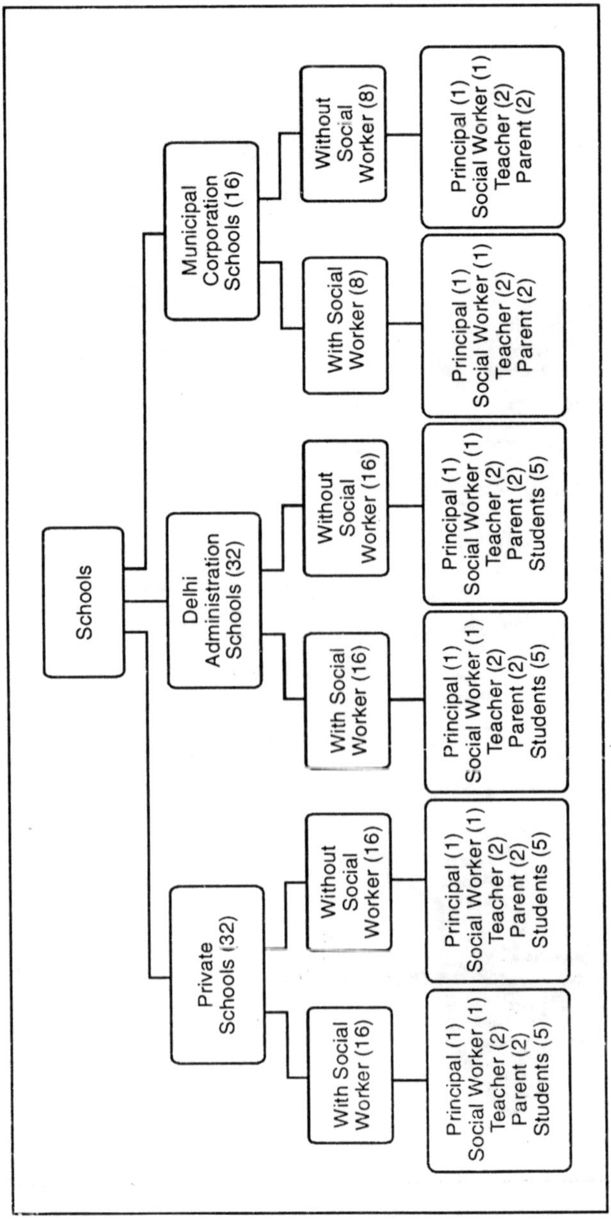

Figure 2.4: Classification of Sample Size

by using stratified random sampling, three types of schools have been taken-up—private (thirty two), Delhi Government Schools (thirty two) and Municipal Corporation (sixteen). Out of which (eight) private, (eight) Delhi Government Schools and (four) Municipal Corporation Schools were taken from each zone. In the second layer of stratification, each type of school has been divided on the basis of presence or absence of social workers. So, out of eight private schools, four with social workers and four without social workers have been included for the study. Similarly, four Government Schools with social workers and four without social workers were included in the sample. And two Municipal Schools with school social workers and two without social workers have been taken-up for study.

Private Schools with Social Workers

There is a wide range of schools with private management. They largely cater to children from economically well-off background. Parents of children in private schools are often educated and professionals. Parents, who send their wards into these schools are commonly aware, understand the worth of education and also give their necessary support to children to develop and learn various skills. In these schools generally the decision of appointing social worker was taken by the management only. However, these schools (having school social worker) are less in number in Delhi. The social workers are having different designations in different schools. So, the researcher decided to take such sixteen schools which do liaison with the community irrespective of the designation of school social worker (four from each zone). But despite of lots of efforts and number of schools visited, the researcher could not be able to find any school having school social work in the East and the North zone. She only got schools with school social work in West and South zone.

Private Schools without Social Worker

Another set of private schools were taken for comparative study that included those not having any post/designation like school social worker or any equivalent to it. They were many in numbers, but the researcher took sixteen from them (four from each zone) as sample which suited best to represent all.

Government Senior Secondary School with Social Worker

These were the schools that come under Delhi Administration. It may be noted that very miniscule proportion of such schools were having school social workers. Only five schools were having a post of social worker all over Delhi. These posts got dissolved with the retirement of the designated person. So, the researcher could not get much option and could able to find only two of them (one was from South zone and other was from West zone) as three posts were vacant. Except this, the Delhi Administration School of Delhi Government were having the post of counsellors and they were little more in numbers, approximately 72, as told by one of the counsellors during the study. The researcher also took the views of five counsellors for the research.

Government Senior Secondary Schools without Social Worker

In this category, Delhi Administration Schools were included where no social workers are employed. They largely cater to economically disadvantaged children, the children who are generally the first generation learners. Actually, Administration schools are the feeder schools of Municipal Corporation Schools and generally the children of these schools come from low economic background or lower middle class. The schools were many in numbers, but researcher selected sixteen of them from different zones (four from each zone).

Municipal Corporation with Social Worker

Municipal Corporation is an autonomous body. Now, it has been trifurcated, namely under these—

S.D.M.C.—South Delhi Municipal Corporation
N.D.M.C.—North Delhi Municipal Corporation
E.D.M.C.—East Delhi Municipal Corporation

All of them having their own hierarchy to manage respective Municipal Corporations. South Delhi Municipal Corporation also includes West Delhi Municipal Corporation. The researcher took two schools having social worker from each zone (as mentioned above). For that the researcher had to visit schools, which was a tough task as well as time consuming.

Municipal Corporation without Social Worker

In this, the researcher included those schools which are not having social worker. Although they are large in number, but the researcher included only two from each zone. These are the schools, which cater to children largely coming from low economic background. Generally, the parents of these children have migrated from other states in search of jobs and most of these children are first generation learners.

Criteria of Selecting Schools

The researcher took two criteria of selecting school—

1. The school should be recognized by the Directorate of Education.
2. The school should be functional at least since the last five years.

Data Collection Units

From each selected school, principal, one social worker (only in schools with social worker), two teachers (senior teachers), two parents (whose children are studying there for the last five years) and five students (senior students who are studying there for the last five years) were covered in the study. But in Municipal Corporation Schools only principal, one social worker (only in school with social worker), two teachers (senior teacher), two parents (whose children are studying there for the last two years) were included. As students are too young to answer to researcher's questions, they were not included in the study.

The study was designed with the purpose of developing in-depth understanding about pupils' perception and the school environment among the schools with social worker and those without social worker.

The study is primarily qualitative in nature with many socio-demographic variables to be studied quantitatively. Sampling was purposive in nature as the researcher required to gauge the suitability of the school for gathering information.

Tools and Techniques of Data Collection

Primary Data

To collect empirical information from various units, the researcher mainly relied on interview guides. Interviewing technique has many advantages, some of which may be explained in the study context. One, during interviewing, information gathered can be verified by means of observation, which was particularly relevant in the present study. Two, at times, the respondent may not be able to understand the question, which can be reframed and posed again. Doubts can be clarified thereby reducing the dropout of cases, which are very frequent in the case of mailed questionnaires. The researcher developed interview guide for the following data units:

- *Interview guide for social worker*—This contained questions like their roles (inside and outside school), challenges faced in carrying out roles, status they receive, rapport with teachers and students etc. A large number of questions were kept open-ended from general to specific ones. All remarks of respondents were captured to get in-depth information on the subject.
- *Interview guide for administrative head*—An interview schedule was used for administrative head as they are in a position to give opinion regarding the social work programme and the social worker. The principal acts as the bearer of all important components of the school, that is, children, parents, teachers and management. The questions in the interview schedule were kept open-ended to understand the perception of the role of School Social

Worker and social work programme by the administrative heads of schools having school social work. And in schools without school social worker, questions were aimed at knowing the administrative head's opinion about the school social work programme.

- *Interview guide for teachers*—An interview schedule for school teachers contained questions on their perceptions about the scope of social work in school setting. And in schools without social workers, questions were on how the teachers are catering to the mental health needs of the students and what they feel about the school social work programme.
- *Interview guide for students*—School students were interviewed to appraise their views on the role of school social worker in the school system. In schools without social workers, questions were aimed at understanding the implicit and explicit needs of school social workers as viewed by the students.
- *Interview guide for the parents* –An interview schedule was used for the parents also. The questions in the interview schedule were structured to understand the knowledge of the parents about the school social work programme, their perception about the programme and the role of school social worker.
- *Unstructured Interviews/Discussions/Correspondence*—Unstructured Interview discussions and correspondence with significant people (like people from various NGOs who are working in various schools, as a single unit) associated with the functioning of school social work, were taken into consideration. This was done to get in-depth information on the topic at hand.
- *Observation*—Observation has been used as supportive tool to check consistency of the information gained through interviews.

Secondary Data

In the study, secondary data were collected from different libraries like Jamia Millia Islamia Library, NCERT Library, JNU Library, Department of Social Work, DU Library, and IGNOU Library. In addition, digital search or the Internet usage was also done to collect relevant information.

Data Collection

The data collection was done into three stages, which are as follows:

Formation of Sample Frame

In this, list of schools (both private and government) was procured after much hard work, contacting Directorate of Education and Personal visits in both kinds of schools (private and government).

This hard work resulted in—

- Gathering list of Government schools having social worker.
- Gathering list of Government schools not having social worker.
- Gathering of list of private schools having social worker.
- Gathering of list of private schools not having social work.

Selection of Schools

In this the researcher first divided the universe in four zones, namely—East, West, North, and South. Then she selected the schools as sample for research, on the basis of zones. In this, sixteen private schools having social work (four from each zone), sixteen private schools not having social work (four from each zone), sixteen Government schools having social work (four from each zone), sixteen Government schools not having social work (four from each zone), eight Municipal schools having social work (two from each zone) and eight Municipal schools not having social work (two from each zone) were included in the study.

Collection of Data

In this all important people associated with or without school social work like administrative heads, teachers, children, social workers were contacted personally or through correspondence. All efforts were continued throughout the study and the reports and other relevant materials were procured. Apart from this, records and reports concerned with school social work were taken into consideration. The collection of data was not an easy process as the researcher had to face following problems especially in Government schools:

- Firstly, to contact the social worker of Government schools, the researcher first had to find out the schools having the post of school social worker, which was really a tough task as the numbers are very few. This consumed a lot of time of the researcher.
- Secondly, to contact and interview social workers of Government school required efforts. There were hindrances from the side of the schools, as administrative heads suspected that the questioning might lead to unfavourable criticisms of their functioning. Only after clarifying the facts and after much persuasion, the required permission was granted.
- Thirdly, unavailability of the respondents due to various reasons also delayed the process of research.

Data Analysis and Interpretation

For this study, primary and secondary data were integrated to get adequate and in-depth understanding of the subject. The data were analyzed into different themes and then comparisons were made between schools with and without social workers. Comparative analysis was also done between Government and private schools in relation to having or not having social workers. Wherever required, findings were represented in the tabular form.

Report Writing

The dissertation is divided into six chapters. Chapter one 'Introduction' provides the research argument, history of school social work in different countries and in India, and models of school social work. Chapter two has review of literature, objectives and research methodology. Chapter three discusses the comparative description of private schools, both with and without social workers. Chapter four gives scenario of Government schools in terms of social workers' roles and functions. Chapter five consists of analytical underpinnings of school social work in private and Government schools on various parameters. Chapter six presents the conclusions and suggestions.

Conclusion

This chapter provides a comprehensive review of literature on challenges faced by schools in terms of pupil's, personal problems, teacher's attitude and constraints signifying the importance of school social workers. The literature is also reviewed on studies showing positive impact of school social workers. The gaps in the literature review were highlighted. The chapter also covers detailed information about the research methodology, which was applied to accomplish the research. In the next chapter, findings of the study specific to private schools are delineated.

References

Adams, A. (1996), *Even basic needs of young are not met.* Retrieved from http://tc.education. pitt.edu/library/SelfEsteem.

Adeyinka, A.G. (2009), *Marriage and Family in Changing Society*. Ilesha: Wanday Press Publisher.

Agarwal, R. and Kapoor, M. (1998), "Parent's Participation in Children Academic Activities in Relation to their Academic Achievement at the Primary Level", *Journal of Indian Education*, Vol. XXIII (4).

Barnard, W.M. (2004), "Parent Involvement in Elementary School and Educational Attainment", *Children and Youth Services Review*, 26.

Battle, J. and Lewis, M. (2002), "The Increasing Significance of Class: The Relative Effects of Race and Socio-economic Status on Academic Achievement", *Journal of Poverty,* 6(2).

Bhatnagar, A. (2012 May), *The Challenges that Indian Teachers Face when Seeking Employment at International Schools and how to Overcome them*. Retrieved on May 10, 2015 from http://teacherhorizonsblog.com/2012/05/08/the-challenges-that-indian-teachers-face-when-seeking-employment-at-international-schools-and-how-to-overcome-them/

Bolusteve, F.N. and Sanni, W.O. (2013, March), "Influence of Family Background on the Academic Performance of Secondary School Students in Nigeria", *Life Psychologia*, Vol. 21, No. 1.

Bowen, N. (1999, January), "A Role for School Social Workers in Promoting Student Success through School Family Partnership", *Social Work in Education,* Vol. 21, No. 1.

Bowen, N. and Bowen, G.L. (1998, October), "The Effect of Home Micro-system Risk Factors and School Micro-system, on Student Academic Performance and Effective Investment in Schooling", *Social Work in Education,* Vol. 20, No. 4.

Bowers, Swithun (1952), "The Nature and Definition of Social Case Work", *Principles and Techniques in Social Case Work,* (ed.) Cora Kasius, New York.

Bronstien, L.R. and Kelly, T.D. (1998, July), The Multi-dimensional Approach to Evaluating School Linked Services: A School Social Work and Country Public School Partnership, *Social Work in Education,* Vol. 20, No. 3.

Crosnoe, R., Johnson, M.K. and Elder, G.H. (2004), "School Size and the Interpersonal Side of Education: An Examination of Race/Ethnicity and Organizational Context", *Social Science Quarterly,* 85(5).

Gandhi, A. (1990), *School Social Work*, New Delhi: Commonwealth Publishers.

Henderson, A. and Berla, N. (1994), *A New Generation of Evidence: The Family is Critical to Student Achievement*, Columbia, MD: National Committee for Citizens in Education.

Hussain, Ch. Abid (June, 2006), "Effect of Guidance Services on Study Attitudes, Study Habits and Academic Achievement of Secondary School Students", *Bulletin of Education and Research*, Vol. 28, No. 1.

Institute of Medicine (1989): *Children and Adolescents with Mental, Behavioural and Development Disorders: Mobilizing a National Research Initiative*, Washington, DC: National Academy of Sciences.

Joshi, S. (1996), *Child Survival, Health and Social Work Intervention*, New Delhi: Concept Publishing Company.

Kumar, M.L. (1989), *Attitude of Teacher and Students Towards School Social Work Programme*, Unpublished M.Phil. Dissertation submitted to Department of Social Work Jamia Millia Islamia University.

National Mental Health Programme (1982), New Delhi: Ministry of Health and Family Welfare, Government of India.

National Policy on Education (1986), New Delhi: Ministry of Human Resource Development, Department of Education, Government of India.

Peck, R.F. and Mitchell, J.V. (1962), *What Research Says to the Teacher Mental Health*, Washington, DC: American Educational Research Association.

Reddy, E.V. (1995), *Primary Education in the Web of Poverty Culture*, Paper presented at the International seminar on School Effectiveness and Learning Achievement at Primary Stage, organized by National Council of Education Research & Training, July 17-19, 1995.

Roberts, G.A. (2007), The Effect of Extra-curricular Activity Participation in the Relationship between Parent Involvement and Academic Performance in a sample of Third Grade Children, *UT Electronic Theses and Dissertations*. Retrieved from https://www.lib.utexas.edu/etd/d/2007/robertsg1'186/robertsg 11186.pdf

Saxton, J. (2000), *Investment in Education: Priv.'te and Public Returns*, Retrieved from http://www.house.gov/jec/eaic.pdf

Trecker, H.B. (1955), *Social Group Work: Principles and Practices*, New York: Association Press.

Walberg, H.J. (1981), A Psychological Theory of Educational Productivity, In F.H. Farley and N.U. Gordon (Eds.), *Psychology and Education*, Berkeley, CA: McCutchan.

White House Conference on Child Health and Protection, *Preliminary Committee Reports*, New York: Century 1930.

WHO (1996), *Life Skill Education in Schools*, Geneva: Division of Mental Health, WHO.

3
Private Schools and Social Work

Private schools which are heterogeneous groups largely cater to economically better-off children and the children who are generally not the first generation learners. These schools consist of wide spectrum of schools where parents are aware and understand the worth of education and also give all necessary support to their ward's education. The Education Commission (1964-66) popularly known as the Kothari Commission, divides the private schools in three broad categories.

(i) **Independent Schools**—They are recognized by the State, but do not get grant in-aid. They enjoy high prestige, charge high fee, pay higher scales to the teachers and adopt English as medium of instruction.

(ii) **Recognized and Aided Schools**—They are recognized by the State Government and also get grants-in-aid. They have their private management, but run predominately with State funds. Their linkage with local community and loyalty of teachers are their main assets while their financial position is their weakness due to uncertainty of Governmental funds.

(iii) **Unrecognized Schools**—They are neither recognized by State Government nor receive any grant-in-aid for running education process. For such schools, Education Commission (1964-66) has stated "some do useful work, but others make a negative contribution to the society".

The sanction to the existence of private schools in India has been given in the provisions of our Constitution. Various articles related to this are stated below:

- Article 30 states that "all minorities, whether based on religion or language shall have the right to establish and administer educational institute of their choice."
- Article 28 (1) and (2) states that all citizens shall have the freedom to establish private educational institutions in order to provide religious instruction of their choice.
- Article 19 (c) and (g) provide freedom to form associations or unions and to practice any profession or carrying on any occupation, trade or business, which obviously provide freedom to an individual or group to establish and conduct educational institutions of their choice.

So, these are some liberal Constitutional provisions that have led to the establishment of a large number of private schools and now the situation is that they become an indispensable part of our education system. No doubt, they are contributing well in the field as stated by the Fourth All India Educational Survey (1982) that they provide better physical facilities for example furniture, laboratories etc. in comparison to the Government Schools. It also says that primary and middle schools are better placed in pupil-teacher ratio in comparison to public sector.

Today private schools are playing an important and commendable role in the development of education in modern India, this could happen because of their flexibility and being open for various new experiments as their greatest assets. This has enabled some of these schools not only to take some bold experiments/steps, but also open a way for others. And the greatest example for this was that of the school social work services which were first introduced in private schools.

Though, private schools mainly cater to the children of middle and upper class families, with the recent notification, 25 per cent seats are reserved in these schools for children coming from Economically Weaker Sections (EWS). This has brought newer challenges in private schools to integrate children from EWS category with other children.

The range of issues social workers in private schools deal with are varied and differ from the challenges encountered by their counterparts working in Government schools. In private schools, social workers come across numerous issues related to family non-functioning and its impact on child's scholastic performance, relationship constraints, pressure of meeting high parental expectation, examination stress, peer pressure, drug-addiction, and so on. Social workers also take-up career counselling, sex-education and dealing with turbulent stage of adolescence. Few social workers are also making conscious efforts to sensitize teachers, Principal and Para-teaching staff about the problems faced by the disadvantaged and disabled children so that they empathies their situation and behave well with them. The social workers also sensitize the children about various social realities and motivate them to help the needy. For instance, during data collection, one school social worker employed in a private school mentioned the following episode :

> The school authority called one of the prestigious cook as a resource person in the school and the cook shared his experiences with the children that he used to cook especially for poor people once in a week and distribute the prepared food items to the road side people. The same strategy was adopted by the school. They made a group of students who came to school on a holiday (scheduled before) and cooked for poor people (raw-material of it has been denoted by school students themselves) and then they distributed the prepared items among the poor people.

So, the scope and content of social work programme differ with the different type of schools like private schools need to focus on individual problems and sensitizing about social realities, while Government schools require work on children dropping out of school, long absenteeism, ill health and providing financial help, etc.

Gandhi (1990) mentioned in her book "*School Social Work*" that in spite of providing a commendable quality of education system these (private) schools are many a time criticized by their detractors for breeding arrogance, exclusively rewarding academic achievement, capitalistic socio-economic system, individualism etc. It is ironical, but true, that maximum new experiments and innovative ideas in education system come from these private schools. This is summed-up by the Kothari Commission (1964-66) which states that—

> "Some form of private enterprise has made a negative rather than a positive contribution to education at the same time we should recognize that private enterprise had played an important role in the development of education in modern India, that a large number of our good institutions are in private sector and that it can continue to make a useful contribution to the development of education in the years ahead."

Expansion of Social Work Programme in Private Schools

According to Gandhi (1990) with the increasing enrollment of social work students in colleges of social work, the requirement of social work agencies had also been increased and the school began to be seen as viable fieldwork agencies. Similarly, on the other side few private schools began to see the utility of the service which can improve the quality of education they are providing to the children. This led to the placement of social work students in schools. And when increasing number of schools started employing school social workers and realized the significance of their services, this led to expansion of the field of School Social Work in Delhi.

The credit of School Social Work programme in Delhi goes to the Delhi Branch of Indian Association of Trained Social Workers from the year 1969.The Association collected funds, gave subsidy and technical guidance to the workers appointed by it in number of schools till they were firmly established. Later on some other schools started coming forward on their own for the employment of social workers. Likewise few voluntary organizations, such as "*Ankur*" helped in the expansion of school social work. They appointed and provided salary to the school social workers for doing community services through school children. This increased the number of schools that introduced social work and gave a better beginning to the School Social Work in Delhi.

It may be restated that social work education has been adopted from the West and hence in the initial years, concentration was on the clinical model of school social work which involves case work and counselling services.

D'Souza (1965) has written about the role of school social workers in private schools. He maintains that "the main role of school social worker is that of an enabler in helping the children, restoring their functioning and to rehabilitate them. Through the case work method he/she helps individuals in making a satisfactory school adjustment."

Gandhi (1990) notes that the implementation committee laid down the scope of school social work programme which includes various aspects of children's problems, as follows :

(i) "Irregularity in attendance and school dropouts.
(ii) Slow learners—not necessarily due to low Intelligent Quotient (IQ).
(iii) Poor children, problems due to inadequacy of funds.
(iv) Children whose behaviour differ considerably from the group—timid, isolated, withdrawn, over-aggressive, sullenness, resentfullness or inability to accept teacher's authority or demand for special attention.
(v) Children who are not making normal progress in accordance with their capacities.
(vi) Children who show sudden deterioration in their work—the reason for which cannot be readily understood.
(vii) Children who come from a home situation known to be complicated.
(viii) Stealing, truancy, fighting, children who become disciplinary problems for teachers."

The social worker not only provides solution to the above mentioned problems, but also gives counselling to the parents and teachers. Except this, he/she organizes programmes on family life education, camps to inculcate desirable qualities in children.

The focus of school social work programme largely remains on problem solving of individual students, until the recommendation for introducing Socially Useful and Productive

Work (SUPW) as a part of syllabi came by Government of India "Review Committee" in 1977. The SUPW contains two kinds of activities in it, one is "production-oriented work" and another is "service-oriented activities". So, the private schools also make use of the syllabi of SUPW to make their students productive and service-oriented, and the work has been done under the supervision of school social worker which not only led to employment of school social workers, but also changed the scope of school social work.

With this basic background, it is relevant to see the existing school social work programme in the private schools and also to compare the necessity of programme in today's perspective with the findings of the study.

Private Schools with Social Work

Given below is the profile of eight private schools from the South and West Zone having school social work. It may be noted that no schools with social work was found in the East and North zone. The findings are thematically arranged and based on the interviews of the respondents done by the researcher. Following schools were included in the study:

> All the eight schools of Delhi were running school social work programme independently. Out of these, five schools were run by Christian Missionaries and three were not based on any particular faith. All the schools were of Higher Secondary level and had a good reputation in the society [based on the *Times of India* rating, 2014]. The teacher-student ratio in all the schools was almost same—either 1:30 or 1:35.Together they had approximately 11,520 students on their rolls.

All the schools had spacious and beautiful building, playground, indoor games hall, adequate library, comfortable furniture, special provisions for special need children as all of them provided integrated education facilities. Three of them had a separate section for special need children with all kind of facilities present. According to them, they first got admitted as per their level in these sections then after learning up to a certain level they move to the main school. For this regular sessions are being taken with teachers, students, and Para-teaching Staff. These sessions help in the integration of special children and care is taken so that none of the children feel alienated, lonely and left out.

For one month teacher from special school also sits in the class with the child at the time of integration to help the new teacher to understand the child and also to facilitate the child in adjusting in the class. Motto of integrating the special child is to make the child aware about the outer world as he/she has to face the world afterwards. But for this they are charged with higher fees which can be afforded by elite group only. All special services and facilities are charged and parents have to shell out money to avail the same for their children. This apart, the schools have certain percentage (25% approximately) of seats reserved for economically backward children. In the EWS category, schools take those children whose parents could not afford the fees. The normal fee ranges from ₹ 3,000 to ₹ 8,000 per month for a child.

School Social Worker

The school social work programme was carried out in these schools by eight social workers (one worker in each school), but one of them got assistance with the concurrent placement of social work students of DSSW. All the social workers interviewed are on the pay-roll of the school and none is getting fund from any other source for appointing social workers.

Let us look at the socio-demographic profile of the school social workers in the private schools. Age of all social workers ranges from 25-45 years and all of them were women.

Four of them have the designation as "School Social Worker", three are called the HOD—Head of the Department [Social Work] and one social worker is designated as counsellor. The counsellor has almost the same work profile as the school social worker. In the findings, all the social work professionals are termed as "School Social Workers" irrespective of their specific designations in their schools.

Findings further show that six of the eight social workers were post-graduate in Psychology, one of them in Social Work and one in Education. They graduated from various colleges, and the one who was post-graduate in Social Work was from Delhi School of Social Work. Their work experience ranges from 1 year to 21 years.

In the study, five of the eight social workers were getting the salary grade of TGT (Trained Graduate Teacher) with various allowances and only three were getting PGT (Post-Graduate Teacher) grade with allowances. All of them are on permanent basis and on a full-time job and all of them have to report about their work to their respective Principals.

Work timings are different for the respondents. Seven of them have to stay 2-3 hours more than the school timings depending on the work, that is, up to 3:00 to 3:30 PM while one of them remains there up to 5:30 PM.

(i) Task Performed by the School Social Workers

Based on the findings of the research, listed below are the various tasks performed by school social workers, which are clubbed under broad headings—

1. Helping children having problems.
2. Making arrangements for open classes or vocational classes in the school for outsiders.
3. Organizing education enrichment programme.
4. Administrative work.
5. Fund Raising.
6. Parent-Teacher related tasks.
7. Organizing income generation programme.
8. Making layout of new projects.
9. Liaison with outside agencies.
10. Organizing camps.
11. Adoption of a community.
12. Briefing and sensitizing teachers and school staff about their work.
13. Sensitizing students about social realities.
14. Handling social welfare projects.
15. Making arrangement and preparation for various awards.
16. Non-administrative work.

(a) *Helping Children having Problems*

From the initiation of school social work programme helping children having problems was given the top most priority by the private schools and the school social workers. The profile of the children seeking and gaining education from private schools may be described briefly. Most children are from economically better off families. Parents of the children are professionals, in service class, or in business and they understand very well the significance of education for their children. So, the problems related to poverty, ill-health, malnutrition, huge family size and difficulty in meeting basic needs, are not found in these private schools. However, with 25 per cent seats reserved for children coming from Economically Weaker Sections, social workers may have to deal with problems linked with poverty and malnutrition. Further, in private schools, social workers usually focus on "emotional disturbances", learning problems, scholastic backwardness due to familial problems, on inter-personal relationships, absenteeism etc. They also cater to children with special needs.

The children with problems are taken as "client" by the social workers and during their interventions, social workers use case work and group work approach depending on the nature of problems.

The school social workers also refer cases, if required, to different professionals and experts, often outside the school. The social worker collaborates with various outside agencies to become not only resourceful, but also makes use of them whenever needed, for example, referring to the psychologist if the child is having any psychological problem.

Findings show that social workers are easily accessible to students and often times, on facing any problems they themselves approach the social work unit in their school. They have been able to establish credibility and visibility in their respective schools. Sometimes, teachers refer cases to the social worker. Reportedly, a couple of social workers also find out children needing help and start interventions with them without waiting for the teachers or parents to refer to them.

In addition, their daily presence in schools facilitates their rapport with children and they approach to them whenever required without any hesitation.

Study results show that on an average, a social worker handles 7-8 major cases in a year, requiring long-term interventions while there are numerous minor cases, which are short-term, that she handles per annum.

For handling these cases the worker freely took assistance and advice of various experts like psychologists, speech therapists, special educators etc., whenever needed and when an expert advice from outside the school is required for the child, the parents were advised to pay the fees of the expert. The parents of private school children are cooperative and they generally escorted their children to child guidance clinics as and when directed by the social workers.

From the beginning of the case till follow-up, the social workers remain in constant touch with the child guidance clinic, parents and child, either personally or through phone. They not only pay home visits, but also seek regular updates on the case from other professionals. They maintain detailed records and monitor the progress of the case.

The researcher asked the social workers about the extent of helping children with problems. Social workers responded that in most of the cases (85%) positive results of their interventions are

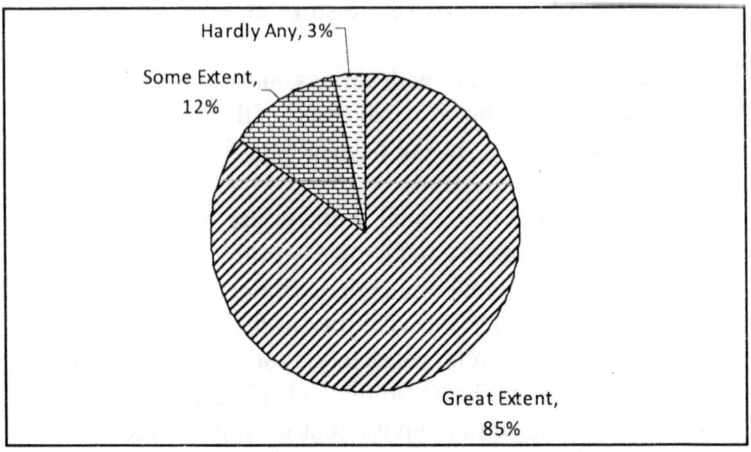

Figure 3.1: Extent of Helping Children with Problem

visible. Only in 12 per cent cases, they are able to help to a certain extent and merely in 3 per cent cases, they are not able to make dent into the children's problems. Figure 3.1 has the details.

(b) Making Arrangements for Vocational Classes/Open Classes for Outsiders

Results of the study show that all the eight schools have adopted one or two communities in the nearby area of the school. Social workers in the schools organize various programmes and courses to improve the quality of life of slum people. They hold programmes such as holding health camp, health awareness campaigns, cleanliness awareness, literacy awareness programme etc., which are need-based and specific to their communities. Under the supervision of school social workers, the students go and do community service. In two of the schools under study, social workers have organized courses in the school premises itself for the community people. The courses were in accordance to the convenience of the school and community people. Most courses are run after school hours. At that time, classes get over and the community people also get free from their work. The schools also provide free transport facility for the community people. One school uses its resources effectively by collecting community people for classes while dropping students to their homes. So, it saves not only time and energy of the people, but also ensures participation of the beneficiaries. Courses for the community people were as follows—

- Beauty Culture.
- Stitching Classes.
- Computer Classes.
- Literacy Classes/Adult Education.
- Open School Classes. (Making school as a study centre for open school students and providing them space and study material there so that poor beneficiaries also get some support in their studies).

The most of these courses aim at making the poor and marginalized community people self-reliant and facilitating in generating self-employment. Although the schools charge fees from the community people, but the amount is minimal. Every course has limited duration like Beauty Culture is of 3 months and scope for advance course is also provided. The schools are getting very good response for their courses and every year huge number of children and adults from the community are passing out and getting certificates of course completion.

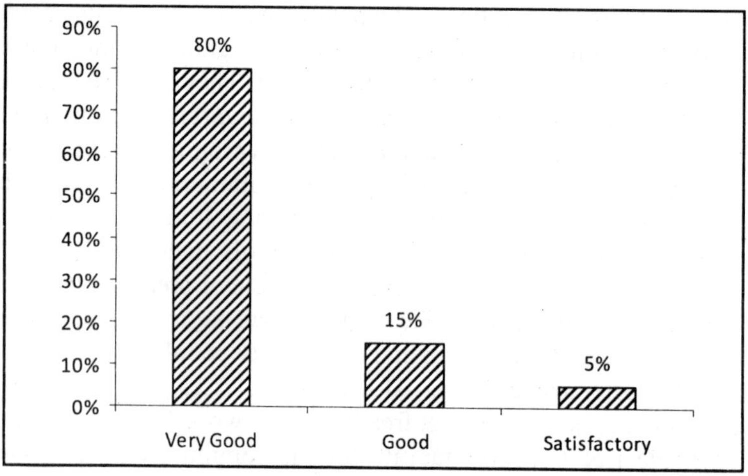

Figure 3.2: Level of Satisfaction for Facilities Provided for Adopted Community

In the study, social workers informed that 80 per cent of the community people are highly satisfied with their community interventions. Another 15 per cent reported schools' role as 'good' and 5 per cent to the satisfactory level (see Figure 3.2). None of the clients from the community has felt any dissatisfaction over the work done by the school (through social workers) in their areas. The researcher corroborated the information provided by the social workers through her own interactions with the community people while she was in the respective schools for her data collection.

(c) Organizing Educational Enrichment Programme

In the study, findings show that the school social workers organize educational enrichment programmes to enhance the educational inputs of the school. The details are as follows—

(i) Socially useful and Productive Work (SUPW)

Initially before the formal induction of SUPW in the school syllabi, some of the private schools were offering this for elite groups, so as to expose them with social realities and do some productive work. But introduction of it opened up a new area where school social worker could make use of their skills and display their quality of work. SUPW constitutes two salient components.

(a) *Production-Oriented Work*—Work which results in production of tangible and consumable 'goods' by using various skills.
(b) *Service-Oriented Work*—Work which is done for the benefit of the community and for developing a sense of awareness among the people.

SUPW is now a part of all these eight schools under the study and each school is trying to give optimum exposure to its students in both services by giving them choice to opt, yet each school developed its own combination of activities, depending upon its resources, manpower and its identified priorities. All the eight schools introduced SUPW activities according to the board requirements and provide exposure to pupils for 6 periods a week at secondary stage (IX-X class) and 4 periods a week at senior secondary stage (classes XI-XII).

In all the eight schools under the study, school social workers play pivotal role in organizing and managing all activities of SUPW, though with the support of the principal and a couple of senior teachers. The schools organize SUPW activities under various clubs or houses and the students opt for these clubs or houses according to their interests. Specific time slot is given in the time-table for the club activities. Students attend their clubs according to their options, and all clubs run their activities simultaneously. Various clubs are health club, cleanliness club, remedial teaching club, etc. The school social worker coordinates the programme and looks after the day-to-day implementation. For this she has to—

- Plan activities of SUPW.
- Coordinate various activities.

- Liaison and supervise the teachers in-charge.
- Evaluate students time-to-time.
- Organize and implement the orientation programme for teachers and students.
- Maintain records.
- Provide briefing and counselling for various activities to parents and teachers of SUPW.

Below are some activities which come under production-oriented work and services-oriented work—

(a) *Production-oriented Work*
- Chalk and duster making
- Educational Aids
- Knitting
- Tailoring
- Typing
- Gardening
- Music and Dance
- Textile Designing.

(b) *Service-Oriented Work*
- Hospital Service
- Blind Welfare
- Library Service
- Canteen Service
- Cleaning the School
- Remedial Teaching
- Health and Nutrition Education
- Non-Formal Education
- Village Camps
- Helping in Crèches
- Fund Raising.

These activities no doubt are useful for the students. Gandhi (1990) also wrote in her book "*School Social Work*" that the Production-oriented activities give a sense of evaluating the actual quality of produced goods, marketability and the efficiency with which the total production procedure had been mastered. For the service-oriented activities, students develop an "ability to think and reason" inculcate qualities of leadership. Such activities enhance "development of students' attitudes and personality". But these skills and abilities can only be developed if the work has been carried out sincerely. To know the effectiveness of SUPW, the researcher talked to some students who were the part of this (SUPW). The following verbatim provides insight into the students' views about SUPW in particular and exposure provided by school social worker in general. Some of the comments given by them were as follows:

- "I was never exposed to such people (poor). No doubt, I saw them on roadside, begging etc., but never viewed them the way I view them now. At that time I used to hate these people, but now I want to do something for them."
- "I used to waste my food very much, meaning I use to throw it in the dustbin, if I don't like to eat, but now I taste it first and take only which is enough for me because it always reminds me that there are many who do not get even one meal a day."
- It helps me to realize the value for money like raising funds for them (poor people) is really difficult task. Now, I started saving money for my own.
- I use to get angry and yell at others if the Air Conditioner of my room was not set right, but now I do not do so because it reminds me how these people live without any facilities.
- This year, on Diwali, we enkindled homemade candles, which made my mother proud on me.
- Making educational aid is really helpful in learning something new.

The researcher found that although these SUPW activities are useful for the students, but still many students face resistance from few parents and teachers. Some parents who value academic achievements more than anything else and the teachers who considered SUPW as "*Faltu ka kaam* (waste of time)" de-motivate the enthusiastic students. So, to avoid these resistances, the schools have made SUPW a compulsory subject for all and have started grading it. This has increased the seriousness among students regarding the activities of SUPW.

(ii) Special Education Programme

Out of eight schools, three schools were conducting integrated education programme. These three have their own separate unit for mentally and physically challenged children. The aim of running these classes separately is to educate the children with special needs at their own pace and then later on try to integrate them with general children. Although one of these three schools had already integrated their 40 such students in the mainstream education after giving intensive academic inputs which is remarkable. While the other five schools have integrated slow learners and partially deaf, short sighted children and children have slight mental retardation by providing least restricted environment for them such as constructing ramps, making them to sit in front row or front desk, providing them with various aids etc. Three schools which have separate special education programme are undertaking following activities:

- Taking case history of children to know the severity of conditions.
- Maintain records.
- Provide regular medical check-up.
- Counsel the child and parents for facilitating integration of the child.
- Liaison with other agencies and resource persons for them.
- Organize programme for parents to give them expert advice to handle their children.
- Fund raising.
- Teach slow learners.
- Counselling principal, whole staff, students, fourth class employees and everyone who so ever is related to the child or in contact to the child.
- Liaison with outside agencies to procureemployment for the handicapped children.
- Provide case work and group work services.
- Motivating parents to be a part of their learning process by calling parents for taking classes once in a week (specially educated parents).

For conducting these activities, they have a separate staff, which includes special educators and counsellors, but this service is only for elite group in both schools, because according to them this service includes lot of expenditure which the school cannot bear alone.

Except this the school social workers organize seminars for vocational guidance, especially for classes IX and X students in order to facilitate selection of suitable course by children. For this they call experts from various fields or carrier guidance counsellors. They also organize various programmes on diverse topics, such as 'family education', sex education, gender sensitization etc. These programmes are not only for students, but also for the school staff, from higher authority to lower level, as even they need to be sensitized about the challenges of life.

(d) Administrative Work

In administrative work the school social workers use to maintain records of their work in different areas like case work reports, group work reports, annual report, making layout for new projects, reports of seminars conducted, special project report etc., which they have to submit to the principal from time-to-time. These records are helpful for them for future reference and also to see the growth in a particular area. Also when they do planning for next year, they evaluate their previous projects and programmes, make reports for awards, etc. Side-by-side one social worker also orients and supervises the work of trainee social worker placed for concurrent fieldwork in the school.

(e) Fund Raising

The school social workers raise funds for various purposes like for helping the children from economically weaker section or starting any new projects (in case the school provides less money for the same). Under fund raising programmes various range of resources are tapped from local sources such as cash, clothes, medicines, old books of students to be given to the needy ones. Social workers also motivate children to make best out of waste materials so that they also learn to conserve environment by recycling and reusing goods. These materials are then sold and money collected is utilized for the proposed activities. Students raise resources for any calamities faced by people anywhere in the country, and the collected materials are handed over to the needy people through some NGOs or individually by the school.

The social workers not only raise the funds, but also maintain records of it so that transparency can be maintained. All work is done with the permission of principal. The way of raising funds, totally depends on the skills and ability of every school social worker, and everyone adopted different ways and modalities for this.

(f) Parents-Teacher Evaluate Tasks

Maximum work of social worker in school setting is related to the students, teachers and parents. So, he/she has to be in regular touch with them. They attend staff meetings, brief about their work to teachers so that their cooperation can be sought, and act as a link between students and teachers, sharing each other's feedback. They voice out the problems faced by the students in front of the teachers and principal and present their reports. They seek opinions of teachers about various programmes projects initiated by the social work unit of the school.

This apart, the school social worker remains in regular touch with the parents also to counsel them, to brief them about the projects, for fund raising and for solving particular cases etc. She also liaises with teacher and parent to resolve their cases. The principle is kept in the loop for all the activities.

In the study, social workers of the private school stressed that coordination is a huge task they carry out on daily basis. Even for supervising the SUPW related activities, they coordinate with the teacher in-charge of SUPW activities and students. They also coordinate activities and interventions with staff members and student-mentors working with children with special needs.

In addition, social workers reported that even the teachers are coming to them with their personal and professional problems that increase their stress levels and seek advice. Teachers do catharsis and burst out their emotions and the social workers handle it in a right manner, which in turn helps the students in providing a relaxed teacher. Moreover, social workers also act as a connecting link between teachers and the principal. They voice teachers' concerns on certain matters in front of the principal so that congeniality can be maintained between teachers and principal.

(g) Organize Income Generation Programmes

Income Generating Programmes (IGPs) are meant for the community people or for the physically and mentally challenged people. All the eight schools have involved in income generation programmes like candle making, providing the needy people computer training, beauty culture, stitching classes etc. The motto of this was to provide these people a skill so that they can become economically self-reliant. Two schools out of eight schools take nominal fees for the same and the classes are held either in schools (after school timing) or in the community itself.

(h) Layouts for New Projects

All the eight school social workers make layouts for the projects. For this they make a report under the following heads: Name of Project.

- Why the project should be launched?
- Aim of the project.
- Who are the parts of the project?
- Target group.
- Duration.
- Resources needed.
- Expenditure on the project etc.

After making layout the social worker consults it with the principal and finalizes the report. Then she executes the project after getting approval from the principal.

(i) Liaison with Outside Agencies

All the eight school social workers liaise with the outside agencies for various reasons, like for referring cases, for fund raising or for collaborating on different projects, for expert advice etc. According to them it is very much important for the worker to be in touch with various organizations working in diverse fields of social work. Secondly, liaison also makes the social worker resourceful and keeps her updated on various social issues. The more resourceful the social worker is the more successful she is in her work.

(j) Organizing Camps

All the eight school social workers organize camps from time-to-time on various social issues like health, education, sanitation, etc. They are organized not only to create awareness among the community people, but also to develop a sense of responsibility among the students who participate in the camps. One respondent social worker said, "To make another person understand, a person has to understand the things thoroughly". So, involving these students is to make them understand about the matter/issue thoroughly and as the children are future nation builders, so making them aware is important so that they will create awareness among others. It is like "*Ek teer Se Do Nishane*" (killing two birds with one arrow).

(k) Adoption of a Community

In the study, all the eight schools have adopted one or two communities, nearby their school with the motto "either take school to the community or bring community to the school". Because schools are the inseparable part of community so it is important that both move simultaneously. Every school has different projects running in their respective communities like literacy, awareness, vocational training, counselling services etc. For this they involve their students in doing various works. The schools have basically adopted the slum areas so that children realize the manifestation of impoverishment and there is a lot of scope to work to ameliorate the conditions of slum dwellers. This not only boosts the confidence level of school children, but also makes them aware of social realities and develops feeling of brotherhood and compassion.

(l) Briefing and Sensitizing the Staff about their Activities

It is very important work because if a teacher is aware of the various activities of school social work then it will be easier for them to cooperate with school social worker and participate and contribute to the programmes running in the school under the gamut of social work unit. Secondly, it is helpful for creating better understanding between teachers and the school social workers.

Social workers, in the study maintained that it is important to orient and sensitize teachers about our programmes so that their cooperation can be sought. Sensitization is needed from lower level to higher level like from grade IV to the level of Principal. One school social worker cited that, "if we are working with children with special needs then, everyday we try to boost their confidence level by doing various things as their confidence level is very low. A single comment like "*yeah toh pagal hai* (he/she is mad) given by a Para-teaching Staff could spoil all our work". Sensitization sessions involve each and every member of the school.

Findings bring out that out of eight schools, only one school is organizing sensitization sessions properly and formally. The other four schools are sensitizing in an informal way like discussing the issue while sitting in staff room, etc.

(m) Handling Various Social Welfare Projects

All social welfare projects come under preview of school social worker, so for this the social worker has to do each and every work like making blue print of projects, estimation of manpower required when the project starts, planning and execution of the project. Apart from this, supervision and evaluation of the project are also the part of the social worker's responsibilities. The social worker is the one who looks after the progress of every social welfare project.

(n) Preparation for Awards

To enhance prestige and credibility of the school, the social worker has to make various reports and submit them for different awards at the inter-school levels or State or National levels. This work not only brings pride to the school, but also provides good recognition to the work of social worker.

(o) Non-administrative Work

Findings show that all the eight school social workers have been involved in one or more, small or big non-administrative work of the school. As one of the social worker mentioned, "Being a part of school you have to get involved in these (non-administrative works) also as others are doing it." Below is the list of non-social work:

- Taking various classes as substitute teacher quite frequently.
- Taking subject classes.
- Invigilating during examinations.
- Checking examination papers.
- Looking after school discipline, etc.

Although school social workers make use of their substitute periods to discuss or to engage them or encourage them in any productive work or undertaking guided group interactions on any relevant issues, they cannot rely on these "free periods" to provide life-skill education to students. They definitely need structured allocation of periods or time slots in the time-table.

(ii) Job Perception by School Social Workers and Role Strain

It is very much important to know how the school social workers perceive their present job. Do they enjoy this work? Do they feel comfortable with the school management? Do they find recognition in school? Are facilities provided to them adequate or not? Can they execute their own ideas on sensitizing children or involving them in social work activities in the school? If not what are the ways to improve their present functioning.

Findings show that all the social workers in the private schools under study enjoy their work. Good rapport with the school authorities is one of the salient factors contributing to their job satisfaction. As one school social worker said "if you have better understanding with the higher authority then nobody can say anything to you." According to them they put their views openly and discuss the issue at hand in a healthy manner. All received cooperation from a large number of teachers, but three of them admitted that at sometimes they do not get cooperation from parents (as they give much importance to academic work instead of these activities) and they have to convince them thoroughly.

As far as their training is concerned, seven of them admitted that their friends (who are related to this field) in social work or psychology help them in their present job. One social worker who was from education background affirmed that she was provided with learning opportunities by way of participating in seminars or in-service trainings.

All the eight social workers were satisfied with the infrastructural facilities in terms of separate room, place for the group activities, stationary provided etc.

All the social workers, reportedly, enjoy their job, but occasionally they are overburdened. When 3-4 projects are simultaneously running and there is shortage of manpower, social workers do feel exhausted. In those times, they find themselves unable to do record-keeping and report writing. They all admitted that teacher can only help them to an extent, but organizing, managing, evaluation and supervisions are the tasks of school social worker, which is not only tiring, but sometimes frustrating as well. They also agree that it is a part of their job and they have to do it.

Findings bring out that all the social workers are not facing any problem in their jobs, but when asked, all gave some or the other suggestions for the better functioning, which are as follows—

- More awareness among people about SUPW activities.
- More publicity on role clarity for the role of school social worker among people.
- More job opportunities and compulsory vacancy in all schools and job security.

More awareness or special seminars on the role of school social worker for principal and school staff.

(a) Cases Handled by Social Worker

Problem—Depression

Anil (name changed), student of class 10th was average in studies. But, before three month from Board Exams he took so much stress that he lost his confidence and came under depression. He was in so much depression that he could not be able to solve small and easy sums of Math. The Math teacher referred the case to the social worker. She consoled by say "getting good marks does not mean a successful life neither one set of exams are the criterion of judging one's calibre. There are many students who are good in studies, but could not able to perform up to the mark due to various reasons like health problem. But, this does not mean that it is the end of their lives. Exams are conducted to see the understanding level of student not make him depressed."

By taking continuous sessions and encouraging the child, the social worker able to help out the child to overcome his depression. And Anil did reasonably well in his Board exams.

Problem—Behavioural

Sarita (name changed) was a student of class 7th of a private school in Delhi. She was below average and an aggressive child. On trivial issues she used to get angry and beat other children of the class. The class teacher referred the child to the social worker. The social worker made rapport with Sarita and took some sessions with her to know her problems. She got some links as her brother used to study in the same school and was brilliant in his studies as well as in other co-curricular activities. The social worker paid home visit and got to know that Sarita gets less attention by her parents as most of the attention was taken by her brother. The social worker handled the case very well by taking sessions with the girl, her parents, concerned teachers and with her brother and made them realize that being a child she also needs attention. Now, she is still average in studies and has become less aggressive.

Problem—Adjustment

Bharti (name changed), is a student of 11th class in a private school and is having good academic records. Everything was going well, but before her final exams she met with an accident and could not give her exams as she was on bed rest for about five months). That made her repeat the class, but it affected her significantly as she saw other class mates sitting in 12th standard and she was sitting with her juniors. That deteriorated her academic performance too. The class teacher referred the case to the social worker. She took various sessions with the girl and her parents to console her. She was made her understand that there are many students who themselves drop their year to get admission in various institutions. So, losing a year is not a big deal. And that was an accident because of which it happened to her otherwise she is good in studies. So, in this way social worker helped her in adapting to the situation.

Problem—Complex

Anita (name changed) is a student of class V. She was an intelligent child and one year back she got admission in a reputed school under 25 per cent quota for Economically Weaker Sections. But in continuous two assessments she got very less marks. She also remained quiet in the class. The class teacher discussed the matter with the social worker. The social worker took three to four sessions with the girl and found that she felt inferiority complex with other children as she comes from the lower economic background. This factor not only created complex in the child, but also developed hesitation in her. The social worker took individual sessions with the girl, joint sessions with the teacher and the girl, and organized various activities to make her mingle with her class mates and made her comfortable in the school environment.

Problem—Health

Porush (name changed) is a student of class 4th in a reputed school in Delhi. The boy was suffering from some kind of skin problem. Though the problem was not communicable, but many a times he suffered from itching in between the class and at that time he had to apply oil on that portion. According to the doctor, he will overcome with this problem after 2-3 years. Although he was a brilliant child, his class teacher observed that he is losing interest in the studies and started sitting alone in the class. He also stopped taking initiative in the class. She discussed the matter with the social worker. Social worker suggested to her to find out the reason as being class teacher it would be easier for her (as the children were small). The class teacher came to know that his class mates tease him because he could not do many things due to his skin problem like swimming, playing in mud etc. The teacher informed the same to the social worker. The social worker studied the case in depth. First she built-up confidence and acceptance of the problem in the child. Alongside, she took session with the class on the day when he was absent. She cautioned the teachers, Para-teaching Staff, students, not to make him feel rejected. In all this, she also involved the parents as they would also help their child. This apart, the social worker also organized activities in which Porush mingled with other class mates. With the efforts taken by the social worker, the child again improved in his studies, started making many friends and was able to come out of his problem.

(b) Researcher's Observation

In spite of the fact that the school social workers were totally satisfied with their jobs, the researcher still found certain challenged faced by the respondents. There is no role clarity among the teaching and non-teaching staff of the school with regard to the social worker and hence, they are asked to do multiple and ambiguous roles as per the school specific requirements. Although they claimed that they had good rapport with principal and staff still their suggestions have shown that they are struggling for their identity. The reasons could be the lack of awareness about the role and scope of social work and single post of school social work in the school. As a result, their problems are not fully understood by others in the school and if they have to fight alone to carve an identity in the school system, which is a difficult task. However, all the school social workers admitted that they met with other school social workers sometimes in various seminars and programmes etc., which gives them strength, satisfaction and support, which they could not get from the teachers of their school. Such kinds of meetings with peers help them in sharing their experiences, learning from each other, getting ideas for new projects, discussing complex cases etc., along with unwinding.

Opinion of Principals about School Social Worker

Being the head of the school it was important to take the opinion of Principal about school social worker and their tasks. Findings have shown that social workers keep the principal of their school posted with their work progress, ideas and constraints. A series of open ended questions were put to the principals, which were related to the school social work programme, goals, task performance of school social workers, their appointment and job profile, facilities provided to school social worker, about other special staff for helping school social workers etc.

Findings show that the qualification of the principals ranges from M.Phil. to Ph.D. in various subjects and all respondents were women except one. The age of the Principals was up to 55 years.

Findings on the perceptions of the Principals about school social work in their respective schools have been arranged thematically under the following heads:

(a) Awareness about School Social Worker

Study results show that all except one of the eight Principals of private schools are aware of school social worker and her scope of work in the school. In one school, though the social worker does all the tasks-related to social work just like her counterparts in other schools, but her designation is that of a counsellor.

(b) Appointment of the School Social Worker

In all the eight schools, the appointment of school social worker is done by the school management with the consent of the Principal.

(c) Who Initiated the Services

Out of eight schools five were Christian schools. According to them it is the philosophy of Christian schools to do welfare activities and charity since ages, so the Principal was also motivated towards it. The rest three schools were Hindu schools, where the respective Principal is responsible for initiating the service with their experience.

(d) Salary of School Social Worker

The school management of all the eight schools pays the salary of these school social workers as they pay for their teachers. All the eight social workers have to report to their respective school Principal.

There are no guidelines or set to rules that govern the functioning of school social workers in all the eight schools. It is the discretion of the school management and Principal to provide job-description to social workers in their schools. For any new project principal and social worker sit together and work-out what is good and important for the school and the children. Then social workers prepare a blueprint of the project and the principal gets it approved from the management. In case of projects where budgets are big then fund raising is also done by the school social workers.

(e) Facilities Provided to the School Social Worker

Facilities in terms of room, cupboards, transport facility if needed (Transport Allowance), and other things which were needed for their work are given to the social workers in all the eight schools.

(f) Special Staff Assistance

Four schools have the special staff as counsellor, while three schools have special staff as counsellor, special educators and psychiatrists.

One school only had a counsellor who does liaison with the community, and is treated as a social worker in the present study.

(g) Does the School has Integrated Scheme of Education

All the eight private schools under the study have integrated scheme of education.

(h) Benefits School Getting because of School Social Work

The Principals were asked about the benefits of school social work. Combined views of the respondents are enlisted as:

- Children got sensitized towards social problems and social realities.
- Children felt satisfaction to help the needy.
- Children try to empathize with their situations. This can help them not only to become a good and humble citizen, but also live their lives better.
- Children realize the importance of money as they are doing fund raising for economically weaker section.
- Children involve themselves to educate or literate the poor and marginalized. In a way schools are making them better people for the society.

(i) Significance of School Social Worker

All the Principals in the study, when asked can the teachers substitute the work of social worker, strongly negated? According to them, a teacher cannot handle the problems in the way a school social worker can do. They asserted that behavioural problems, interpersonal problems, problems-related to their home conditions, adjustment constraints faced by handicapped children or gifted children etc., are aptly handled by a social worker only. The reasons cited are—firstly, teachers are not oriented to perform social work tasks, social work training is a prerequisite. And secondly, teachers have to complete their syllabus and later check copies of 30-35 students per class, conducting examinations and other related activities for them. This increases the work-load on them, so they, have no time to sit separately with the child and handle his/her problems. One of the Principals said, "We cannot allow teachers to do home visits in any case otherwise who are going to take the class." According to them, teacher commonly handle problems which are not serious in nature, like simple discipline problems, academic problems etc.

All the Principals in the study expressed satisfaction over their social worker's role and performance. They believed that social workers have the requisite quality and capability to perform tasks allotted to them.

On asking their opinion about every school should have social workers, the Principals affirmed providing the reason that it is good for the growth of school as majority of students get benefits of it.

(j) Scope of Improvement

Though the principals were satisfied with the work of their social workers, they offered certain suggestions under the scope of improvement, which are as follows—

- Maintaining cumulative records of each and every child.
- Sorting out interpersonal problems related to teachers.
- Providing value education to the children.
- Carrying out home visits frequently.
- Involving parents in the school activities and ensuring their active participation.

Opinion of Teachers about School Social Worker

Since, school social worker needs cooperation of teachers not only to help out the child in a particular situation, but also for the sustainable growth and development of the child, the opinions of teachers on the significance of social workers in the school setting matters a lot. The researcher asked open ended questions to the teachers as well. For this, the researcher selected two teachers each from eight schools. Sixteen teachers gave their opinion about school social worker of their school. The findings are under following headings—

1. *Awareness about School Social Work*—All the teachers said that they only got to know about it when it started in the school. Initially, they don't understand its value, but after seeing the work of school social worker, they feel it is really important and consider it as important part of school life.
2. Out of sixteen, fourteen teachers strongly believed that school social workers are working as a helping hand to groom the child. And two teachers commented that it totally depends on how the social worker works in the school. Given below were the opinions of the teachers interviewed:
   - "Their work of sensitizing the child really is significant in an inclusive education because they avoid eve-teasing and adjustment problems."
   - "They try to draw out humble part of any personality."
   - "They make a child pursue a positive attitude towards life."
   - "They involve children in various projects and activities which make them empathetic in the real situation and help them in their daily life."
   - "School social worker can act as a bridge between students, teachers, principal and parents."
   - "It depends on the personality of the person (school social worker) if her own attitudes and beliefs are positive, she can work effectively, but if she herself is not motivated then the work cannot blossom. So, social workers must have good personality traits as there are lots of things to do in this field."
3. On asking, all the teachers affirmed that school social workers have conducted training programmes or sessions

on sensitization of school staff. According to them, programmes and sessions like sensitizing the teachers, other staff, home training for parents of children with special needs are organized by the school social worker time to time.

4. Time devoted by school social worker to handle problems—According to the teachers there is no specific time for problems. It mainly depends upon the situation and execution of the problem.
5. On asking whether or not the work of school social worker disturbs your class, four of them replied in affirmation and rest twelve negated. But all the teachers agreed that they cannot avoid it, as it will help the child in long-run and if it disturbs the class a bit, then they talk to the social worker and reschedule the sessions according to their convenience.
6. On asking about the case referrals, the teachers informed that many times, they refer the cases and sometimes the social workers themselves locate children having some behavioural or psychological problems. The process of referral was same for all the schools. Apart from this, since most social workers are working for many years in the school, children themselves approach them.
7. Most of the teachers told that the children are aware of the services of social work in the school. According to them every child studying in 6th standard or above is aware of it. They also try to involve them in various activities as well.
8. Fifteen out of sixteen teachers affirmed the relevance and need of school social worker. They further shared their views, which are enlisted below:
   - "School social worker sees the life differently which normally others are not able to do so. Others are so busy in their lives that they do not have time to see outer world or problems. Even they do not bother because it is not affecting their life. But this kind of service makes us to feel that being part of the society we should not avoid it. They sensitize towards the

realities of life, empathize with others and help them out."

- "They see the life with positive attitude which helps to resolve any problems in most sensitive way or help in adjusting ourselves in the complexities of life."
- "They believe if the child grows with all values then it will definitely help them, which is true also."
- "Teachers can only give temporary relief to the current problem of student, but school social worker can remove problems from its root cause."
- "In today's world parents are so busy and live in a hurry that they do not have enough time to sit with child and teach the values which our parents and grandparents did and same thing happens with the schools also, new pattern of curriculum like CCE comes which makes a teacher very busy throughout the year. So, the children are either learning by themselves, through their peer group and media, which could be good or bad. In between school social worker could act as '*Asha ki Kiran* (ray of hope)' for inculcating values in children."

Except this one who did not agree with the need of school social work, in schools said—"I do not fully agree that there should be a post like this because if a teacher wants then he/she can mould the child in a way he/she wants and may help them out, but what happens now-a-days that we over pressurize ourselves and start making excuses like we do not have time. If any teacher wants to help the child then he/she will definitely take out the time." According to her if you have school social worker in the school, but he/she is also not hard-working then what is the use of the post. So, the school needs a social worker, but the social worker should have all the desired qualities.

Opinion of Students about School Social Work

The researcher also took opinion of students as they are the ones who directly get benefits of the school social work service. For this, the researcher took five students from each school (having school social workers). So, in all she had forty respondents for presenting the views of children about the social worker.

All the respondents gave positive response to the service of school social work. Comments given by them are as follows—

- "We feel proud to educate someone who is illiterate at this small age."
- "Performing '*nukkad natak* (street plays)' and making people aware is really enjoyable."
- "Doing something for the people who are unable to do anything or disadvantaged people really makes you happy."
- "It gives us motivation and a kind of confidence that we can also do something good."
- "It makes us mature and a responsible person."
- "I have never come across people like this (physically and mentally challenged), but now I realize their problems, emotions and feelings and in addition helping them in any way not only satisfy me, but motivates me to do more."
- "Doing this kind of work other than academic works in the school motivate us to come to school daily."
- "Organizing camps or programmes really help us to learn various stalls like fund raising, doing team work, collaborating, coordinating, managing, organizing etc."
- "Doing this kind of work makes us to put a side our egos meaning everyone is helping every one. We forget our differences because everyone has only onething in his mind that we have to do something good for others."

On asking the relevance of SUPW activities from the students, 60 per cent of the students found it highly relevant, 20 per cent said that the subject is relevant, 10 per cent considered as less relevant while the another 10 per cent could not found any relevance in the subject.

On asking about the comfort level of students with principal, teacher, and social worker, the researcher found that 80 per cent of children are comfortable to discuss their problem with school social worker, 15 per cent with teacher and mere 5 per cent with principal.

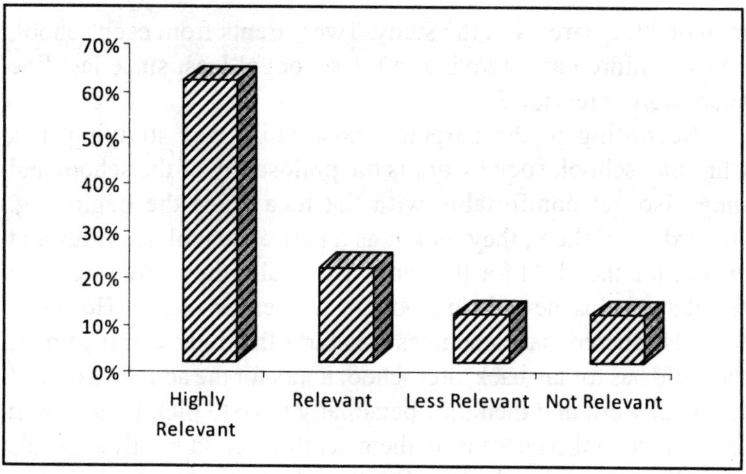

Figure 3.3: Relevance of SUPW Activities

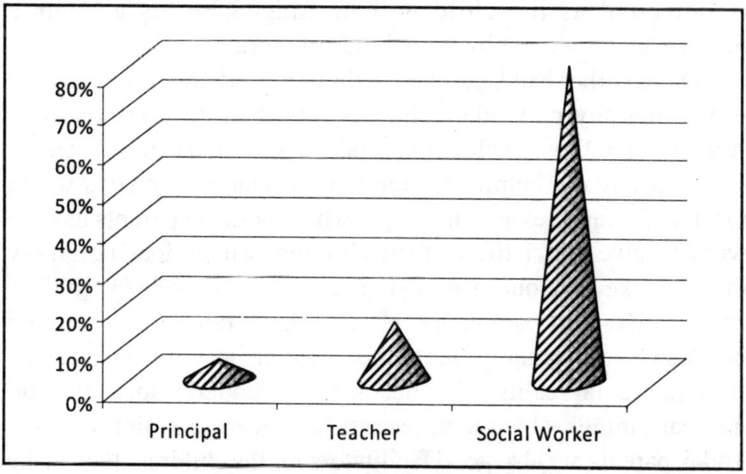

Figure 3.4: Students Level of Comfort with Professionals

Opinion of Parents about School Social Work

Parents being one of the most important stakeholders who encourage their children for involving themselves in social welfare activities, their views cannot be negated. So, the researcher also took views of parents about school social work. For this researcher included the parents in the study. Two parents from each school, whose children are studying in the school at least since last five years were interviewed.

According to the parents whose child was studying in a Christian school, social work is the philosophy of the school and they also get comfortable with the idea since the beginning. According to them, they took it as a part of school activities and encourage the child for the same. No doubt, they agree with the fact that it helps the child in grooming his/her personality. However, they also shared that sometimes it disturbs the studies. Many times, the child has to stay back after school hours for the activities related to social work and then they personally have to pick-up the child from the school. According to them, it affects child's daily schedule as well as parent's schedule. So, they do agree that the activities are good for the child, but at the same time too much involvement is not good as the child will be judged by his academic performances and not by these kinds of work.

On the other hand, parents of children studying in schools not professing any particular religious faith had different opinion. According to them, including social work related activities in the school are really helpful for the child because in today's world most of the families are nuclear, in which both the parents have to work to give better life to their children, which does not allow them to take time out to sit and give valuable knowledge to their children. Neither parents nor children have time to interact and discuss value education. Due to this, children not only remain away from the social realities, but become self-centred also, as they do not learn things which their parents have learnt in joint families. Today parents are also good facilitators for the children; they make everything available whatever the children want so they do not know the value for money. The school social work activities help them to learn about and empathize with people's sufferings and understand that life is not a bed of roses. One has to struggle a lot for this.

Couple of parents had different opinion, but all of them agree the social work service is helpful for the children in grooming their personalities.

Private School without School Social Work

As the number of private schools without school social workers are many, while schools with social work are only few, so to see the difference in them, the research selected equivalent numbers of private schools without school social work. Sample size was sixteen, four schools from each zone.

In schools without school social workers the researcher took the perception of principal, teachers, students and the parents about school social work. For this she asked open ended questions to the respondents. Findings are thematically arranged as follows:

Opinion of the Principal about School Social Work

The researcher covered sixteen schools which are private schools, but without school social work. The principals were having experience of ten to twenty years and had qualifications ranging from M.Ed. to Ph.D. level. All the sixteen schools are equal in almost all aspects (infrastructure and school facilities) in comparison to the schools having school social work. However, when the researcher asked about school social work, all were not aware about the real concept of school social work, whereas in schools having social work unit, almost everyone was well aware of the concept and activities of social work in the school.

Although five of the schools (out of sixteen) have post of counsellor and one school has a club system that undertakes community service time to time. According to them, the role of social worker is done by the teachers. Words quoted by one of the Principals of schools without social workers are "teachers are responsible for overall development of children so the teachers themselves handle their problems, their needs and aspirations etc. They guide them at their level and solve their problems."

Apart this, one school has different corridor system and each corridor has one coordinator, who is a school teacher. These corridors are meant to take-up social welfare/work activities. The coordinator manages the problems of respective corridors and if the problem cannot be managed at coordinator level then it goes to the principal and they together handle it.

When asked, about the time constraints among teachers for club activities, the teachers informed that they have enough time to handle the problems and do all the social work related activities. The teachers handle all these works in their free time or free periods and in zero periods. That was one of the reasons that the schools had not taken any initiative for the post of school social workers. They believe that the teachers especially the class teachers know each and every child of their class and he/she is responsible for the growth and healthy development of the child.

Problem-Hearing

Nikita (name camouflaged) a student of 9th class. She failed twice in the same class. Teachers used to make her sit in the last row of the class (especially at the time of inspection) as she, invariably, would raise her hand to reply, on asking question, but never gave correct answer. One day a teacher called her and asked the problem. Till that time, none of the teachers or any other person has tried to understand her problem. From there, the teacher got to know that the girl is having hearing problem. Nikita could understand the concepts when she was made to sit in the front row as she was able to listen properly. The teacher discussed the matter with her mother, but she refused to consult the doctor as it was a matter of a 'girl'. Instead she said, "*ji padhegi to padhlegi par mein machine nahi lagwaungi kyonki shaadi bhi karni hai. Woh jyada jaruri hai or waise bhi itna to usko sunta hi hai*" (if she is able to study without hearing aid, it is fine, otherwise I will not get any hearing aid…she has to get married, which is more important than studies. As such she is not totally deaf.) Despite enough persuasion, the teacher could not be able to convince her mother. And Nikita continues to suffer from this problem.

Many children due to weak eyesight or hearing problems go undetected and are considered moron or slow learners. Few teachers, due to their sensitivity, are able to detect such problems in their pupils. However, they may not have ample time to persuade parents to consult the doctor. Presence of a social worker in the school would have made the difference in this case and in many such cases.

In the series of open ended questions, the researcher also asked about community service done by the school and about the integrated scheme of education. Findings show that the community service is done by majority of schools, but not in a continuous manner may be twice or thrice in a year like organizing rally on world's environment day, spending one week on cleanliness and plantation in the nearby area etc. Further, majority of schools have integrated scheme of education, but the number of students are not much and the students they are having, according to them, do not need any special educators because they all are minor disabled like having hearing problems, weak eyesight etc., which could be overcome with the help of aids.

Ironically, the scene was different which the researcher got to know by the parents whose one child is of special needs while another is studying in one of these sixteen schools. According to the parent, the school management does not appoint special educators in their school may be to save money and they only prefer to admit those students in their schools who have minor disability. The parent discussed her case with the researcher, and the words quoted by the parents were as follows—

> "I admitted my child in the school (one of these sixteen schools), but there was no special educator. My child is a slow learner, she cannot coordinate her mind with her other body parts so frequently like we do. She was in the same school for three years, but finally I had to take her out, because the school authority did not understand the problem. Most of the time the principal and teachers used to call me and give a list of problems they were facing with regard to my daughter. The class teachers used to say that she spoils the class results as she could not score the marks, but they did not understand that the child needs special attention to perform well. Secondly, how a special need child can spoil the results of a class as according to the rule they should be counted separately from the rest of the class results. I was so fed-up with the school authority that I had to admit my child to another school (having

special educators). Now, I am satisfied with the present school, but in some way increased my work load. As my other child still studies in the previous school and both school timings on same, so I have to rush to collect my both children. When I get late then previous school authority asks me "why you come so late to collect your child? then I tell them "you forced me to do so".

Opinion of the Teachers about School Social Work

To check out reality in the words of principal and to know how a teacher handles the problems and needs of their students the researcher felt that it is important to take the views of teachers working in these private schools. For this, the researcher asked open ended questions to the teachers of these schools. For this, the researcher took two teachers each from the schools according to the sample. In all, she interviewed thirty-two teachers (two from each of the sixteen schools having no social worker).

Findings of the study show that none of the teachers were aware of the concept of school social workers, but they have knowledge of counselling. According to them they themselves cater to the needs of children and solve the problems like behavioural problem, absenteeism. And if they are not able to solve it, then they refer to the counsellor of their schools or outside. According to them they never came across a problem which they cannot handle. For this, one of the teachers said "we are mature enough to handle problems as we also have children and we know the problems a child can come across. A social worker and counsellor will not do any exceptional work; a social worker would also suggest the ideas that we suggest to deal with the problem. She added that my own child had some problems in his studies and the counsellor of the school called me and suggested the ways to help out the child, but I knew all of those and I was applying all of them, but it takes time to cope up with the problem".

Mishandling of Infatuation by a Teacher

A boy named Rohan (name camouflaged) was studying in a reputed school of Delhi in class 10th. He was having an affair with a girl of 9th class of the same school. One day both of them were caught alone on the roof of the school by a school teacher. The teacher, instead of talking them in confidentiality and discussing the matter in a matured way, highlighted the issue so much that everyone in the school got to know about them. They were ridiculed and disdained publically. Their parents were called and questioned on the values inculcated in them. The incident not only affected the integrity and self-concept of the two children, but also disturbed them mentally so much that they could not handle the disrespect and shame. The girl changed her school and the boy, who was otherwise academically very bright, got very poor marks in 10th. Due to this, he could not get admission in any other school and he had to take admission in I.T.I.

A school social worker is well equipped to handle such cases and maintain strict confidentiality. She/he would have dealt with the case in a much efficient and mature way.

(a) Problems Usually Teachers Come Across

According to them they come across with the following problems—

- *Behavioural problems (like indiscipline, irregularity etc.)*—According to them there are large numbers of children in the school and each child is different from the other. To get few in-disciplined children, irregular children, below average children is quite normal thing.
- *Infatuation problems in the stormy age of adolescence*—(which according to them is increasing day by day due to media and other things) and the researcher found that to solve this problem one school principal ordered that the girls and boys will use different stairs in school so that they could get less time to talk even though it is a co-

education school. On asking to the teachers of that school whether this is correct way to handle the problem, they answered that "what will you do then? You have to find out ways in which students have less time to share their feeling." The adolescencc period is a turbulent stage, in which a person is ready to do any act, right or wrong, moral or immoral. If at this age, the person is properly guided then he/she leads a disciplined life otherwise indulge in acts of misbehaviour and misconduct.

- *Adjustment Problems*—According to them adjustment problems do exist when a child enters in new environment and may feel lonely if not well treated, but according to them they get better with passage of time.
- *Bunking classes*—According to them it only happens if the teacher is not taking care of or the child is not having interest in the studies. But it only happens sometime. Teachers put a regular check on it.
- *Smoking*—For this the teachers educate the children from time-to-time that smoking is injurious to health. But according to them they cannot put a check on them every time.
- *Intellectual inferiority or superiority*—Generally, intellectually backward pupils are ridiculed by their teachers and class-fellows in the class so many a times they develop a feeling of retaliation and indulge in abusing and creating disturbances in the class. Similarly, intellectually superior pupils also disturb the class by going out and coming in without permission. As such pupils find no proper channels for the utilization of their superior intellect.
- *Bad habits*—Certain students develop bad habits because of their home and social environment, undue check or control, or maltreatment by family members, economic conditions etc. These bad habits lead to bad behavioural practices of such lying, stealing, abusing, damaging school property, and committing various types of unlawful acts.

According to the teachers, for all these matters they either do counselling of the child or call parents to handle the child or suspend the child for few weeks. On asking how much time they are able to devote to the children for the same, they informed that they take all matters when they have time, but majority of the teachers also said that as they have only few periods free and have other work load as well, they only cater to those cases which get highlighted, rest they avoid. Because according to them, they can only survive in the schools if they give their best to make their academic results fruitful. As quoted by one of the teachers, "teachers are here to teach the students. If anybody evaluates the work of a teacher then they will evaluate on the basis of their subjects and not on the basis how much moral values are provided by the teacher." According to them, no doubt moral values are important, but still they cannot give it much importance as it puts a question mark on their survival in private schools. They shared that to solve any problem from its root needs time and follow-up work, which they do not have. According to them, they solve the problem just on the basis of situation and not for the long-term basis. On this, an example given by one of the teachers is, "It is like a pain killer given for instant relief, but not to cure the problem in long-run." So, most of the teachers act as pain killers for student's behavioural, emotional and developmental problems.

(b) Task Performed by Teachers in Private Schools

In private schools teachers remain busy in the following:

- Maintaining records.
- Maintaining boards/school declaration.
- Preparing lesson plan.
- Organizing and preparing students for functions and curriculum activities.
- Organizing various competition and quizzes etc.
- Making question papers for examinations.
- Editing material for the school magazine.
- Checking papers and copies.

- Conducting examinations.
- Taking substitution periods.

Except this on an average they have to take 32-36 periods in a week, i.e. 5-6 periods per day for a 6 days week, which in turn means they have only 2 periods free from their schedule and in that most of the time they got substitution period.

On asking, is there a need of any specialized person (like school social worker) in the school, all the teachers gave positive response as it makes their work not only easy, but the students can also get benefited out of it, which, in turn, would help them.

Opinion of the Students Regarding Services Provided by Schools

As students are the direct beneficiaries of services from the school, it is important to know their views about social work service and administration of the schools. Although the students of these schools were not aware about the concept of school social work, but they are aware about the services given to them. So, just to know their satisfaction level the researcher put an open ended question to eighty students of these sixteen schools (five students from each school). All the students were of 10th-12th standard and studying in the school at least since last five years. The researcher opted for them as they are well aware about the school services. All of them gave different views. Satisfaction level of students with services is given in Table 3.1.

Table 3.1: Satisfaction Level of Students with Services

	Out of 80	*Percentage*
Fully Satisfied	10	12.5%
Partially Satisfied	14	17.5%
Not Satisfied	56	70%

According to Table 3.1, 70 per cent of them showed their dissatisfaction to the service given to them. Following are comments given by them—

- "Counsellor of the school shares our problems with other teachers."

- "Teachers spread the matter if we do anything wrong and labelled us, because of that if anything wrong happens anywhere, the concerned teacher without knowing the truth catches us."
- "The suspension of the child for few weeks is the only punishment."
- "If a girl is talking to a boy the teacher without knowing the reason, would discuss the matter with other teachers and tarnishes her image in the eyes of other teachers".
- "I am not much aware about counselling service as I never had any such session, only the problematic children goes there."
- "Teachers have no personal relations with us, they come to the class take the period and go. They all are doing their work because they are getting salary for it."
- "Our previous counsellor was not so good so everybody was afraid of sharing anything to the new counsellor."
- "Teachers are judgemental because they believe in the gossips they hold in the staff room without hearing the students' perspective."
- "We are at the lowest position in the school, no one listens to us especially the ones who are not good in academics. Teachers are in authoritarian position and they make Principals also to listen them only."
- "I do not want to take science, but because there are only few students in science stream and if I score good marks they (teachers) would convince my parents to enroll me in the science stream."

Except this 10 per cent students are fully satisfied by the school services while 14 per cent students are partially satisfied by the school services.

Opinion of the Parents Regarding School Services

Parents are the prime socializing agent in a child's life and they also influence child's perception towards school's services. No school alone can make the child responsible and sensible citizen, but it is a duty of both parents as well as the school. So, the researcher took the opinion of the parents regarding the school services they are availing for their child. She asked open ended questions to the parents of children having no school social work in their school (private school).

The parents of private school (having no school social worker in their school) were of upper middle class, doing jobs in various fields. Either both the parents or at least one of them are working. Majority of them were not only aware of the importance of education in their child's life, but also give all the necessary support to develop their children holistically. The reason behind this is the fact that "children are their only assets". So, making them educated and good citizen is the sole aim of their life. However, for most parents, "academics" is their main issue of concern. Results show that parents were nominally satisfied with the school services, but when asked about school social work, they were not aware about it. In addition, they had very different impression about the school counsellors also. According to them, counsellors are there to solve the problems of any problematic child and because their children were not problematic so they do not need the services of a counsellor. They think negatively if counsellor calls them, they do not think that it is good for the child development and counsellor is there to suggest the ways to handle a particular child, which shows lack of liaison in the school services with the parents of the children.

Conclusion

In this chapter, the findings related to private schools have been delineated. Not many private schools have social workers. However, wherever social workers are appointed they are involved in myriad of activities and tasks—from solving psycho-social problems of students, liaison with nearby community, integrating children with special needs in the mainstream education, and other administrative tasks. When compared to with schools without social workers, the school teachers are burdened with the additional responsibilities of handling children with problems. Many times the teachers are not well-equipped to perform the "social workers" role effectivcly. This is also confirmed by the interviews with children in both the type of schools. Thus, social workers play critically important role in the school setting. In the next chapter findings of Government schools are presented.

References

Ankur is a Delhi-based voluntary agency which provide grants to the schools undertaking non-formal Education programme through the involvement of school children, under the Guidance of School Social Workers.

D'Souza, C.; Syed, R.; Sonaya, S. (1965), *Social Work Forum*, Vol. 3, No. 2.

Gandhi, A. (1990), *School Social Work*, New Delhi: Commonwealth Publishers.

Ministry of Education: *Report of the Education Commission (1964-66), Education and National Development*, Government of India.

4
Government Schools and Social Work

In 1973 Delhi School Education Act was passed, according to which the responsibility of Pre-Primary and Primary level of education in Delhi was given to local bodies like Municipal Corporation of Delhi, New Delhi Municipal Council and Delhi Cantonment Board. The Directorate of Education was made responsible for Secondary and Senior Secondary level of education. Right now there are 2,400 schools of Senior Secondary level with 17,00,000 students enrolled in it (Directorate of Education, 2015). The Student-Teacher ratio is presented in Table 4.1.

Table 4.1: Student-Teacher Ratio

Level	*Ratio*
Primary Level	1:40
Middle level	1:42
Secondary and Senior Secondary School	1:48

Because of the space constraint, the majority of Sarvodaya Vidyalayas and Municipal Corporation Schools were made to operate in two different shifts, a morning shift for girls and an evening shift for boys. Due to the high growth rate of the Delhi's population and shortage of infrastructure, the Directorate of Education has also introduced primary classes into 364 Sarvodaya Vidyalayas.

These schools are either from 1st to 12th standard or from 6th to 12th standard. Some of them are co-education while the rest have shift system. Morning shifts are for girls and evening for boys. Timings for morning shifts are 07:00 to 12:30 (in summers) and 07:30 to 12:30 (in winters) and for evening shifts are 1:00 pm to 6:00 pm (in summers) and 1:00 pm to 5:30 pm (in winters). Thus, during winters the schools runs thirty minutes less in comparison to summers. These schools are feeder schools of Municipal Corporation of Delhi Schools which means students passed out of Municipal Corporation of Delhi schools get automatically admitted to these schools in next standard. That means the same students goes to these Sarvodaya Vidyalayas. The schools which start from 1st standard have to bear an extra burden as the students coming from Municipal Corporation of Delhi Schools either increases the number of sections or increase class strength. Delhi's Directorate of Education (DoE) is the department under the Education Department of Delhi Government that manages the city's public school system. It is one of the India's largest school education system.

Delhi's public schools have never been known for their good infrastructure, for many years majority of the Delhi's schools even did not have proper school buildings which forced the students to attend the classes in open, or in temporary tin-sheds. Although still there are some schools having tin-sheds and no proper buildings in some schools, but since last 15 years the conditions have changed and with the efforts of Directorate of Education, many schools have received well architecturally developed state-of-the-art buildings and other infrastructures (Directorate of Education, 2015).

The researcher, as per the sampling design, had planned to cover sixteen schools of Sarvodaya Vidyalayas having schools social work and sixteen schools which do not have school social work. She also included both the shifts in her research. Following are the details of Government Schools having school social work—

Schools with School Social Work

Sarvodaya Vidyalayas are also the feeder schools of Municipal Corporation of Delhi schools, which cater children of lower income group (like people living in slums). Because the children are from low income group (LIG) and living in slums, people face lots of problems such as high dropouts, ill health, economic problems, non-conducive family environment etc. are the burning issues. These issues create lots of scope for school social work. In this backdrop, the researcher planned to cover sixteen schools where social workers were working. But after searching a lot the researcher could not be able to find any such post in these schools except two schools. Given below is the profile of those two Government Schools having school social work, which were covered in the present research.

Both schools were of Higher Secondary level and working under Directorate of Education (DoE) with the teacher-student ratio as 1:48 (as mentioned earlier) and with approximately 11,580 students on the roll.

Both the schools had spacious and good, but old buildings, although some classes were running in tin sheds in one of these two schools. Both schools had a playground, a library and furniture (but not adequate). There were ramps for children with special needs, but no separate section for them as their strength was very low. Secondly, the school does not have special educators, although Government provides special educators on contract basis through Universal Elementary Education (UEE) Project. As these special educators are given more than one school to take care of, they lack time and often just come and give technical advice to the teachers to handle children with special needs. Majority of the students coming to the school were from lower castes (like *Dhobi*, *teli* etc.) and low income group, where either one or both parents work for their living.

This apart, facilities like scholarship of SC/ST/OBC students, medical check-up, money for uniform (as per the class), free books up to 8th standard, ₹ 800 for 9th to 12th standard students per head for books, Midday meal for students up to 8th class, money for the SC girl child, aids for children with special needs from various NGOs working in the field, money for stationary, and Ladli scheme etc., are functional in both the schools. The schools charge no fees up to 8th standard and nominal charges like ₹ 30 per month from 9th to 12th grade. No detention policy exists in the schools up to 8th level. The profile of school social workers working in these schools is mentioned in Table 4.2.

Table 4.2: Profile of Social Worker at Government Schools

Age	Ranging from 50 to 55
Sex	Female
Religion	Hindu
Educational Qualification	12th + ITI Diploma Holders
Designation	School Social Workers
Salary Grade	Primary Teacher (9,300-34,800)
Working Timing	7:30 am to 1:00 pm
Job Type	Permanent
Total Experience	Ranging from 30 to 35 years
Reporting to	Principal

Role of School Social Worker

Findings bring out that the scope and duties of school social worker in these Government Schools vary significantly from their counterparts in private schools. During interviews the school social workers admitted that they are only designated as "School Social Workers" (on official papers, they are designated as "Social Education Workers") while their work profile is very different. The actual reality behind their post was totally unexpected. According to them, in 1983, under a project of adult education some ITI-holders and some war widows were appointed. The motive of which was to start various centres at different places to provide varied skills to women along with adult education. All of them (called Social Education Workers) were provided with one-one centre. A small training of art and craft, stitching and vocation courses was given to them to continue the centre. At that time their salary grade was 330-560 and their working timings from 9:00 am to 5:00 pm, that is, full time job.

But in December 2004 the project closed and they were sent to Sarvodaya Vidyalayas. Out of all those only 30 people were appointed in 1983 by the Directorate of Education, as "Social Education Worker". According to them, a clause was there in their appointment letter that Principal of that particular school can take any work out of them matching their ability (to confirm this, the researcher wanted to see a copy of their appointment letter, but the respondents were hesitant and she could not get it). So, right now they are working as substitute teachers, handling different responsibilities, doing any other administrative work or taking primary classes. Their post remains as "Social Education Worker" in the school, but the ambiguity over their job profile did not end here. According to them, in October 2007 the Government tried to transfer all Social Workers under UEE Project, but the refusal of Principals to release them (due to deficiency in staff) saved them to get transferred. Till date they are working in the same school in which they were sent in 2004. The social workers also informed that the post dissolved with their retirement, so only few social workers are left.

From the above mentioned information it is clear that there is no concept of social work in Government Schools, it is just for name sake. Neither the staff designated as social workers are oriented with social work knowledge nor it created any difference in the social environment of the Government Schools. Thus, there is no apparent difference in Government Schools with social workers in contrast to the government schools without social workers. As there is no difference between both the schools (school having social work and those not having social work), the researcher will mention the collective perceptions of both types of school's principals, teachers, students and parents about school social work. Although she covered all schools (schools with social work and school without social work) as mentioned in the sample (in total thirty two), but because the scenario was same so there was no need to mention it separately.

Perception of Principal about School Social Work

The researcher has covered all thirty two schools (with school social worker and without school social worker) to take the perception of Principals. The qualification of Principal ranges from M.Ed. till Ph.D. level and experience ranges from 1 year to 10 years. To take the views of Principals about school social worker the researcher asked open ended questions, but she collaborated them under few headings, which are as follows:

(i) Knowledge about School Social Worker

Out of thirty two only two of them heard about school social worker programme, remaining thirty of them were not having any conceptualization and knowledge about school social work.

In fact they heard it for the very first time, except these two Principals. One of the principals who know about school social work, interviewed informed that he was a teacher in the school (one of the schools under New Delhi Municipal Council), when the social worker were appointed in N.D.M.C. by higher authorities. According to him, school social worker did not do any remarkable job and he mentioned following reasons for supporting his statement:

- The social worker was allocated with a number of schools.
- Due to this, there is acute shortage of time.
- They are supervised by the educationalists, who did not know how to utilize their services effectively.

According to him all these factors created hurdles in the tasks of school social workers and gave a negative impression of their work. Another Principal has heard about school social worker by someone known to him and as he was not in a position to appoint a school social worker in his school. So, he himself tries to perform certain roles of school social worker, like talking to the students about their problems, listening to their concerns, taking remedial classes after school, giving informal education to marginalized street children etc.

(ii) Catering to Mental Health Need and Problems of Students

According to the Principals, teachers themselves take initiatives if they feel that the child is not adjusting properly or feeling depressed or anxious. In such situations, the teacher calls the concerned student individually and counsels him/her accordingly. Each class teacher is responsible for the students of his/her class and intervenes to solve their problems. Moreover, from time to time, Principal of the school also gives lectures on stress management and provides support to pupils and sometimes, to guide them resource-persons from outside (counsellors) are called, especially for class X or XII students.

Problem—Stealing Ill-equipped to Handle Kleptomania

Preeti (name changed) studies in a Government School of Delhi in class 11th. She used to steal money from her teachers' purse and from the students' bags. She was caught stealing many times, but every time, she cries foul and pretends to faint. Gradually, the entire school came to know about it. Teachers and students are clueless regarding handling of the problem. The problem still persists as teachers are not in a position to do anything due to strict laws.

A school social worker would have assessed the problem of Kleptomania and resolved it with scientific techniques of behaviour modification.

Problem—Ill Effects of Peer Influence

Ashok (name changed) studies in 11th standard in a Government School of Delhi. He was average in studies and a well-mannered boy. On the farewell day of 12th class, his friends made him to drink and also provoked him to use abusive language for the Principal. Under the influence of alcohol, he went to the Principal's office and started abusing him. The Principal called-up Police and his parents. However, the matter was sorted out in some way. But, after that incident, his peers and other students started avoiding him and teachers also started scolding him on trivial issues. Ashok now feels lonely, alienated and rejected. He is unable to concentrate on his studies too.

School social worker could have handled the case and would not have let the situation deteriorated.

(iii) Integrating Scheme of Education

As per the policy guidelines, none of the Government Schools can refuse admission to children with disabilities. In Government Schools, invariably each class has a couple of children with some kind of physical, mental or learning disabilities. The school teachers only are handling these children and working on problems related to their integration in the class. Although, under Universal Elementary Education (UEE) project the schools are provided with special educators (on contract basis), but each educator is given six schools to cover. So, it becomes difficult for them to concentrate even on one. So, they come and tell certain techniques and guide the teachers to handle the children with special needs. They also counsel the children, teachers and parents, if required. Apart from this, Government also has started organizing in service trainings or seminars to provide training to the teachers to integrate children with disabilities with the class.

(iv) Community Service or Community Collaboration

The Government Schools do community service only when they get orders from higher authorities. In addition, they motivate students at their personal level to do good for the community like motivating them to do plantation, helping the needy etc. And for community collaboration, the school organizes Parent-Teacher Association (PTA) meeting in which discussions on certain issues like health and hygiene of students, importance of studies, their personal problems etc. is held. Along with these, the school remains open for the parents to come and discuss the problems, if they have any, with the concerned teacher and parents too have scope to monitor the functioning of the school.

(v) Need of School Social Worker

All the Principals do agree with the fact that it creates burden on teachers' working and because of this they affirmed that there should be a specialized person (social worker) who can handle all these problems of students and also does liaison with the parents and community. However, the modality of appointing a social worker with lots of ambiguity in his/her job profile as done by Delhi Government is not the required option, as remarked by the Principals. The Principals (of schools where social education worker was appointed) echoed that appointment of social workers like the earlier ones in Government schools would be futile exercise and there is no use of appointing them.

(vi) Initiatives to Appoint School Social Worker

During interviews, the Principals were asked if they are convinced with the relevance of school social worker, what they would do to appoint one in their school. To this, the Principals replied that they are Government Institutions and each one of them is appointed through a Governmental recruitment process. So, they do not have power for creating any post. They only have authority to inform the department about any vacant existing post, but they cannot create any new post. Only higher authorities have the power to create such a post.

Perception of Teachers about School Social Work

The Principals have told that some of the roles of a social worker are performed by the teachers only, such as handling problems of students and paying home visits in case the student is absent from the school for a long time.

This raised certain queries in the mind of the researcher, such as — Are the teachers really capable enough to handle the problems of students? When do they do home visits, in school time or after school?

- What kind of relationship teachers share with parents of their students and how frequently they meet? Are the teachers able to cater to the problems of children with special needs effectively?

The researcher took thirty-two teachers (two teachers from sixteen schools) according to the sample size. All of them were of TGT or PGT level teachers (senior teachers) who were teaching 6th till 12th standard students from at least last five years. The views given by them were as follows:

(i) Knowledge about School Social Work

All were aware of social work, but not school social work. They knew only the counselling part of it which either is done by the counsellor (if any) of the school or teachers themselves.

(ii) Task Performed by the Teachers

According to the teachers tasks performed by them in these schools are as follows—

- Doing admissions.
- *Distributing money*—The money comes to schools for various reasons from the Government like money for uniform for up to 8th standard, scholarships for minority students for stationary from 9th to 12th standard etc. While distributing this money they also have to maintain records, which hampers the teachers work as parents comes at different times and they have to entertain them sometimes even in the middle of class.
- *Filling up of 'Ladli' scheme forms*—The *Ladli* scheme has been started by Delhi Government for the girls who are born in Delhi. The Delhi Government has fixed a certain amount which will be given to the parents of the girl child at the time when she passes 12th standard. So, forms are filled at various levels like at the time of 1st, 6th, 9th and 12th standards. This consumes time of teachers as they have to see all the papers and then fill up the forms.
- Managing classes as a substitute teachers.
- *Distribution of books*—Books came from the department for the students up to 8th standards, which the teacher has to collect first from the department and then distribute it to the various classes.
- *Mid-day meal distribution*—Mid-day meal is distributed up to 8th standard, which is distributed half an hour before lunch because it is difficult to recognize children during lunch. Whosoever is the in-charge of it, they first have to receive mid-day meal and then do daily routine formalities like filling the daily form of mid-day meal and get it signed by Principal, 2 parents and second in charge, and then distribute the mid-day meal. Although distribution is done by Para-teaching Staff, but presence of in charge is required.
- Handling various charges.
- Editing the school magazines.

- Correcting copies.
- Decorating class boards/bulletin boards.
- *Taking classes*—Every teacher has to conduct 38 to 42 periods on an average in a week, which means conducting 6 to 7 periods in a day out of total 8 periods, leaving only 1-2 period free for other activities. In most of the cases these 1-2 periods are consumed as substitute teacher.
- Making question papers for examinations.
- *Election, census and other Government duties*—These kinds of duties are mandatory duties which normally do not fall on working day, but they do add-up the work load of the teachers especially, common teachers, who are more in number in schools.
- Attending seminars, organizing and conducting Parent-Teacher Meeting.
- Organizing and conducting tours for various classes.
- *Doing administrative work*—One or two teachers (if the staff is big 70-80 teachers) remains always busy in doing administrative work. Although, There is vacancy of three people—one UDC, one LDC and 1 Superintendent in every Sarvodaya School for administrative work, but in many of the cases the posts remain vacant and the work is done by the teachers as reported by one of the teachers).

The teacher, in addition to the above tasks, also works for the new examination systems, i.e. Continuous and Comprehensive Evaluation (CCE). The CCE involves activity based evaluation which puts more burden on teachers as they have to complete the syllabus along with certain other activities for the students. CCE involves lot more tests and assessment on periodic basis including unit tests, FA1, FA2 etc. So, most of the times the focus of teachers remain on either to complete the syllabus or correction of papers.

(iii) Problems Usually Teachers Come Across

The teachers reported some gender aspects in terms of the problems they encounter with their students.

Common Problems which they come across with girl children, particularly, in their respective schools are as follows:

- *Behavioural problem*—Behavioural problems are found among children in these schools are many such as attention seeking behaviour, aggressive behaviour, anxiety, depression etc. The reasons could be—problems in parental upbringing, highly energetic children not able to channelize their energy in a proper way, stressful home environment, unwanted child etc.
- *Short attendance or dropout cases*—According to the teachers, short attendance or cases of dropout varies from individual to individual. But, in most of the cases, if the girl is involved in any moral misconduct or if she shows less interest in studies, or they move to some other place then they dropout from the school.
- *Not taking proper attention*—According to teachers children coming from low income group get mature, much earlier than their age because of their environment which not only diverts their mind, but affects their studies also.
- *Infatuation problem*—The teachers reported that most of the schools are double shift schools where morning shift is for girls and evening shift is for boys. During adolescence, sexual attraction is usual among both the sexes and they get infatuated. Example of this one can see that how girls and boys behave, when morning shift is getting off and evening shift is about to begin.
- *Family Problems (broken family)*—According to the teachers, a large number of children in their classes come from dysfunctional families or broken families. They often belong to lower income-group families where due to space constraints there is no privacy and parental conflict is easily visible. Many times there are financial problems too. This adversely affects the mental well-being of the children.
- *Adjustment problems*—The teachers informed that sometimes the children who are coming from private schools face lot of adjustment problems in the class as they felt lots of difference between both the settings. Here, the children are more rowdy and rustic so, it creates problems for those who are pampered or sophisticated.
- *Eloping with boy-friend*—Due to the curiosity of opposite

sex and their environmental influence girls' take these kinds of steps like eloping with some boy. The teachers come across two-three cases of these kinds every year.

Common Problems which they come across with boy children are as follows—

- *Smoking and Chewing Gutka*—According to teachers, most of the male students above class 9th are indulging in smoking and tobacco chewing. They often find wrappers and burned cigarettes on the ground. Although students usually do not bring cigarettes and Gutka etc., in school premises. They take it before and after the school. However, now-a-days, they have usually started taking "GOLA (a sort of drug)". It is cheaper in cost and makes the person sleepy. It does not create any smell also so nobody is able to know what is happening to the child. Another thing which 6th to 9th class children do, is inhaling white correction fluid, which they spray on their hankies and keep on smelling it. Slowly-slowly they get habitual of it.
- *Alcoholism*—The teachers reported that many students indulge in alcoholism especially of senior classes. Many times empty bottles of liquor are found in toilets, but hardly any one is caught red handed except in few cases.
- *Indulging in Crimes*—The teachers also informed that some students of senior classes indulge in immoral or criminal activities to earn money (as money is always their priority) or for other reasons. These students also bully other students and spoil school discipline.
- *Indulging in bad habits and using abusive language*—The children usually involved in bad habits like playing cards, video games etc. Except this they use abusive language with each other which they learnt from their environment.
- *Short of attendance*—According to the teachers, those students who are doing part-time job, or are the part of bad company, or indulge in any addiction etc., usually have short attendance.

- *School Dropout*—Sometimes because of financial conditions the students have to drop their studies as they have to earn for their family and sometimes their bad conduct plays vital role in forcing them to leave their school.
- *Not giving importance to education*—According to teachers, sometimes student lose their interest in studies because of parental pressure, peer group influence, too much work load (as some student also do part-time job to support their family), lack of facilities, and lack of proper guidance etc.
- *Class bunking*—Although it happens in most of the schools (boys' schools), but where there is Muslim community, its frequency is much higher (especially every Friday) because they have to go for *Namaz*. So, they bunk the classes. Except this, there are many reasons for other students like to make fun, to avoid classes of particular strict teacher etc.
- *Eve teasing*—Many rowdy boys also eve tease and harass girls. Though, it happens outside the school premises, but, if the schools are of double shifts, the problems become acute.

(iv) Problems with Co-education System

Apart from the problems discussed above, in co-education, sexual attraction, stalking, love affairs, betrayal etc., are quite common.

(v) Teachers' Role in Sensitizing and Solving Problems of Children

The researcher, during interviews, asked the teachers what they do to resolve the above cited problems. To this, the teachers from girls' school said that from time-to-time, they themselves listen to the problems of students and make them understand about various sensitive issues either by discussing it in the assembly or at the personal level, whichsoever is feasible.

An example given by one of the teachers is as follows: A student eloped from her home with an unknown lady. She was found after 2-3 days of vigorous efforts by her family members. By

God's grace nothing wrong happened to the child as timely action was taken. In the school, during the assembly, (hiding the name of the child) the episode was narrated to all the students and they were cautioned not to take such decisions that can create troubles for themselves as well as for their families.

Problem—Absenteeism

Reena (name camouflaged) is now in 7th class, studying in a Government School in Delhi. Since, the beginning, she was very irregular in the school. She would come to school only twice or thrice a month or whenever there are examinations. Although, she was not good in studies, but still teachers have to promote her to the next class due to no-detention policy. Teachers called her parents several times, but they never came to school. Teachers are helpless and clueless in this and many such similar cases.

Problems of absenteeism are handled by school social workers effectively in the schools they are appointed. This case signifies dire need of social worker in Government Schools.

In boys' schools, teachers do cater to the problems and issues, but either limit themselves to the junior classes, which are up to 8th-9th level or usually avoid the problem if it concerns the senior level children. According to them, in Government school every second child is a problematic child as they come from lower-middle class plus they are hyper active boys. So, the problems do exist, but a teacher tries to avoid it. Because, if teachers get involved more in any particular case and call the parents of the rowdy children to school, then the students start threatening the teacher. For instance, in one particular case, the teacher scolded a student for not paying attention to his studies in front of the class. In reply, the student said "*Sir Aapko to Uthwana Padega* (Sir, you need to be kidnapped)". The teacher commented, "Who will say anything to such boys" Pretending to be ignorant is the best option.

Secondly, the teachers told that they have orders from higher authorities that they cannot scold or punish any child. Therefore, teachers also allow them to do whatever they want to do or do nothing to stop them. As according to the teachers, "these people (students and their parents) are more aware about their rights not their duties". They want a small issue which can help them to make money like fabricating or giving wrong statements about any teacher and filing a case against him/her and then, asking money to settle down the case out of the court. This is unnecessary harassment for a teacher. So, most teachers prefer going to the school, taking classes and quietly coming back home, overlooking all such problems and ignoring bad behaviours of disruptive students.

For sensitizing the children, teachers informed that they do take issues, like "Smoking is injurious to health" etc. in the assembly time and try to give moral values to them, but according to them students rarely follow their instructions.

This apart, one of the school teachers also shared that they do not have good relations with the Principal (who is directly appointed). According to them, the Principal thinks that he is the supreme power in the school and he can do anything. He usually scolds teachers on trivial matters, during the assembly time, in front of the students. This spoils the teacher's image in the eyes of the students and then they do not listen to the teachers.

To conclude, all the thirty two teachers agreed with the fact that every 3rd or 4th child in the Government Schools is a problematic child. Sometimes, they are suffering from problem or sometimes their environment does not allow them to adjust properly. "Teachers do as much as they can do and rest remains *Bagwan Bharose* (at the mercy of God)", commented one teacher.

(vi) Time Devoted by Teachers on Solving/Issues Problems

Teachers either solve the matter in free time or, if possible, avoid the matter due to following reasons—

- Unavailability of Time.
- Work Overload.
- Unaware parents or sometimes more aware parents who

know their rights, but do not know their duties and responsibilities.

- Non-cooperative Principal.
- Now-a-days, many students especially boys, retaliate any disciplinary action taken against them and even threaten the teachers on it.

(vii) Need of Specialized Person

On asking whether there is need of any specialized person who can cater to the mental health problems of students, then all said 'yes' for it. According to them, if a person like school social worker can help the students then he/she must be appointed.

Municipal Corporation of Delhi Schools

Municipal Corporation of Delhi is an autonomous body which governs eight of the eleven districts of Delhi. It is one of the three Municipal Bodies (the other two are New Delhi Municipal Council and Delhi Cantonment Board) of Delhi and also among the largest Municipal Bodies in the world.

Within its jurisdiction are some of the most densely populated areas in the world. It has also the unique distinction of providing civic services to rural and urban villages, resettlement colonies, regularized/unauthorized colonies, Slum/Squatter Settlements, private '*katras*' etc.

MCD came into existence on the 7th April, 1958, under an Act of Parliament. Prior to that DMC (Delhi Municipal Committee) was the Principal Civic Body of Delhi. Eminent Freedom Fighter Guru Radha Kishan has the honour to represent MCD (initially Delhi Municipal Committee) for a long duration as a Councillor. The first elected Mayor of Delhi was Aruna Asaf Ali and Pt. Trilok Chand Sharma served as First Mayor of Delhi. Since then, the Municipal Body has always been alive in its constitution and functioning to the growing needs of citizens. The 1993 Amendment of the Act brought about fundamental changes in composition, functions, governance and administration of the corporation.

Recently, the Municipal Corporation of Delhi has been trifurcated, namely—

North Delhi Municipal Corporation
South Delhi Municipal Corporation
East Delhi Municipal Corporation

Although Municipal Corporation of Delhi schools do not come under the researcher preview, but because majority of staff in Sarvodaya schools come from Municipal Corporation of Delhi schools, so we cannot ignore it. Not only students, but the teachers also when get promoted join Sarvodaya schools. These are the schools which generally have shift systems wherein morning shifts are for girls and evening for boys. Timing for morning shifts are 07:00 am to 12:30 pm (in summers) and 08:00 am to 1:00 pm (in winters) and for evening shifts timings are 1:00 pm to 6:00 pm (in summers) and 1:00 pm to 5:30 pm (in winters). There are also some schools that are in general shifts (i.e. one shift) whose school timings are 8:00 am to 1:00 pm.

Majority of students in Sarvodaya Schools (Delhi Government School) come from Municipal Corporation of Delhi Schools. As Sarvodaya Schools are the feeder schools of Municipal Corporation of Delhi schools, means, after fifth standard the child is automatically get admission to the nearby Sarvodaya school for further education. So, it created curiosity in the researcher's mind to find out how Municipal Corporation of Delhi Schools cater to the mental health needs of the children. To see the scenario the researcher covered sixteen Municipal Corporation Schools (eight with social work and eight without social work) of Delhi schools. These were the schools up to 5th standard having teacher student ratio 1:40. The schools comprise Principal, teachers, students and a couple of Para-teaching Staff (helpers). There is no clerical staff in any Municipal Corporation of Delhi schools. All clerical works are done by the teachers such as sending the attendance of students to their department, making their salary bills from computer, handling various charges, checking mails, sending information on various issues etc. In some schools buildings are not appropriate and classes are taken in tin-sheds or in tents (in an open ground). The students who came to these schools are generally from nearby resettlement colonies or slum areas. The children usually live in unhygienic conditions, suffer from frequent water-borne ailments and those health problems resulting out of unclean surroundings. These children do not have proper clothing and even have shortage of study materials.

The tasks performed by teachers in Municipal Corporation of Delhi schools are as follows—

- Doing Admissions.
- *Filling-up of "Ladli? Scheme Forms* — This consumes time of teachers as they have to see all the papers and then fill-up the forms.
- Conducting Classes.
- Preparing Lesson Plans/Writing Diaries.
- *Handling Charges*—Each teacher have to take one or two charges like bill charge, boys fund charge, service contingency charge etc. and they have to maintain and work to complete the charge to keep it up to date. Few of these charges require daily management like TV records, radio record, daily attendance and mid-day meal, for which they have to keep track of how much of a food came, which variety of foods came, how many students will take food etc. There are few charges which can be completed on monthly basis like library record, boy's funds, science contingency, monthly statement etc.
- *Distributions of mid-day meal*—This is the responsibility of all teachers including Principal to check the meal first then distribute it. Although, every school has one or two mid-day meal distributor according to the strength, but if the school do not have, then the same work is done by teachers and some of the senior class (Vth) students. This takes approximately 45 minutes everyday.
- Organizing School Functions.
- *Preparing Students for Sports*—Every school do not have special teacher like drawing, music, sports etc. Only schools which have ten sections in total are eligible for getting special teacher. But from years back, no fresh appointment has been made. So, there is shortage of special teachers in many schools even in those which are eligible for getting special teacher. Because of that teachers have

to prepare students for various zonal level competitions, which consume time of regular teacher.

- *Maintaining Records*—Maintaining records is a very hectic and lengthy task because there is lot of details which higher authority wants on regular basis. For example list of 5th class students with all details, list of scholarship students, list of minority students etc. Teachers have to maintain all these records manually.
- *Handling 2-3 classes at a time*—If there is shortage of staff, which is common in most of the schools because in these schools all students come from slums or lower-income group, one of the reasons which is increasing population. The Government order says that one cannot stop admissions, effectively which makes student-teacher ratio irrelevant and create an imbalance. Except this, if one of the teachers is on leave, then they have to combine the class and the number of students in the class goes from 35-40 to 80-85. Managing almost 80 students in one single class is a tedious task.
- *Attending Meetings related to their charges*—Teachers have to attend the meetings relating to their charges during normal school hours and for that they might have to go to another school. These meetings happen almost every month.
- *Distributing books, copies, uniforms and shoes*—Government provide free uniforms and books to the children so that it can help in decreasing the dropout rates. These uniforms and books are to be distributed to students and records have to be maintained. Sometimes, the uniform comes in the form of clothes and the teachers then have to cut the clothes in pieces as per the standard size of the students and distribute it. The teacher is not allowed to hire any outsider as they are not allowed to pay him from the school funds. This issue does not end here only, as then they have to handle parents, who either comes with complaint or a request to change the cloth citing one or another reasons. This happens with most of the parents as

they are economically weak. This also gets repeated in the case of distribution of shoes to the students. For shoes the teachers also have to measure the size of each student. Department gives standard size for each class. For example, 6-7 size comes for class 1st but there are students of 8-9 years in class 1st and they got different sizes which create problem. In such cases teacher has to collaborate with other class teacher and this process involves lot of time and paper work. Although how the rule came that the admission of the child has to be done on age basis means, if the student is of 6-7 years of age then the student has to be admitted to 2nd class rather than 1st class. It does not matter whether the student has studied previous classes or not. This also creates more problems because teacher with such a busy schedule will find hard to take time out to teach such students. The child also is not able to cope-up as there are examinations every 2-3 months. The situation becomes more complex because of no detention policy, which says no student should fail up to 8th standard. How can a teacher award or give passing marks to such students who hardly know even the basic minimum level, it becomes a big question and if any higher authority comes for inspection, they ask questions to student according to class standard/level, which is natural, but it is very hard to manage such a scenario (*Source*—Various Teachers of MCD Schools).

Municipal Corporation Schools with Social Work

Municipal Schools are of two types of arrangements—One is double shifted (in which morning shift is for girls and evening shift is for boys) and another is general shift schools. The researcher covered eight schools (two from each zone) having school social worker. In Municipal Corporation Schools, social work is done with the collaboration model. There are various Non-Governmental Organizations (NGOs) which collaborate with these schools to work with children. For instance, SARD (Society for All Round Development) is working in South and West Zones of Delhi,

PRATHAM and KATHA are working in North Zone while PRATHAM is also working in East Zone.

PRATHAM

The Organisation collaborates with Municipal Corporation Schools with an aim to improve reading, writing, and basic arithmetic skills of children in the age group of 6-14 years. For this, the NGO's three programmes are functioning in various Municipal Schools of North and East Delhi. They are as follows:

- *School based Library Programme*—In this a "creative corner" is developed which is filled with child friendly equipments and books. There library related activities are done with children enrolled up till primary grade. For this two trained volunteers of PRATHAM assist the school in a week for three days each. School supports the programme by providing space for creative corner, pooling their own collection of books with PRATHAM's collection and providing basic furniture and stationery items. The main aim of this programme is to motivate the children to read by variety of activities like making collage with waste materials, thumb painting, paper folding etc. As the children coming to MCD Schools are usually from families of first generation of school-goers and most of them do not possess books of their own nor they get an environment to cultivate the habit of reading, such a programme is very useful.
- *Science Programme in MCD Schools*—PRATHAM, in collaboration with MCD Schools, has been working in two different zones to make two Science Centres functional. This provides an opportunity to the children of class 4th and 5th to learn the basic science concepts through demonstration and experiments.
- *Early Childhood Education Programme*—PRATHAM in collaboration with north MCD Schools runs an early childhood education programme with an aim to assist the

MCD teachers in pre-school activities. The programme is operational in the 30 schools of north MCD.

KATHA

This NGO has been working in the areas of children's education, teachers training and book publishing since 1988. KATHA, partnering with Sarva Shiksha Abhiyan (SSA), has taken a programme called I LOVE READING COMPAIGN (ILR) which aims at kindling the joy of learning among children. It sets up libraries and trains teachers to bring its unique education method into Delhi Government Schools. The programme is working in 50 MCD Schools with plan to roll out into 500 schools within next 5 years.

SARD (Society for All Round Development)

The UK based NGO is working with the collaboration of Municipal Schools in South and West Delhi. They have thirty schools in all with two trained staff members in each school. They make a group of thirty students of slow learner in each school. The basic motive of this collaboration is to help out slow learners in their academic work. They usually stress on Hindi and Mathematics.

As all the NGOs working with the schools are having educational motives and having no liaison with community so the school authorities are not exposed with the scope of social work in community school liaison. The researcher did not get any difference in the views of Principals and teachers having and not having social work in their respective schools. So, the findings that are presented below contain the perceptions of Principals and teachers from all the sampled schools with and without social work (sixteen in all).

Perception of Principals about School Social Work

The perception of the Principals with school social work is more or less same as the perception of the Principals without social work. Both the Principals were not aware of school social work. In the schools where there is NGO's collaboration, the Principal was only aware of their working. The only statement given by most of them was "*ye log slow learners ko padhate hain... ye log kitabe dete hain*" (they teach slow-learners...they provide books). They were not aware of anything beyond this. According to the Principals, they were instructed to allow the NGOs to teach or give books in their schools by the higher authorities.

The Principals of these schools are J.B.T. or M.A., B.Ed. and all of them were promoted to principal (no direct recruitment) so, they were never oriented about school social work in their service. All of them were between 52-59 years and having experience ranging from 1 to 9 years. Issues discussed with the Principals are under the following headings—

Community Liaison—On this, the Principals said that they organize parent-teacher meetings from time to time to discuss various issues related to children with parents. Secondly, they also have School Management Committee of fifteen members for making school environment more supportive and beneficial to the students. It constitutes one Principal, two teachers, one member from NGO (if working in the school), rest are parents of school children.

Catering to Mental Health Needs of Children—The Principals informed that teachers themselves cater to the needs of children as teacher remains the class teacher of the class till 5th standard so he/she is aware of each and every child of his/her class.

Handling Children with Special Needs—According to the Principals, they are few in numbers and have nominal problems like hearing defect, physical disability etc. For that the Education Department gives free aid and as far as facilities are concerned, they have ramps etc., for them. Few of them also said that usually they avoid admitting these children by making the parents understand, as they do not have special staff and attendants to handle these children. Though according to them some special teachers are appointed on contract basis by higher authorities, but each one of them were given many schools to cover which becomes difficult for them to give any fruitful results. So, they started coming and guiding teachers the way of handling these children, but that is worthless.

Relevance of Social Worker: The researcher asked whether or not there should be any post of school social worker, the Principals, in unison, replied in affirmation. They said that if it is beneficial for the children's development then it should be there.

Perception of Teachers about School Social Work

Teachers in Municipal Schools are E.T.E. to M.Phil. in which females are in morning shift and males are in evening shift while both we can see in general shift. In these schools the teachers are over-burdened with various responsibilities like making salary bills, helping parents in opening children's accounts, scholarship distribution, maintaining records etc. Along with this, every teacher caters to at least forty students of a class and if one of the teachers is on leave then other has to adjust the class with her/his class and the number exceeds to eighty students at one time. Shortage of teachers remains yet another problem in these schools as told by one of the teachers.

To know the working conditions and the perception of teachers about their jobs and mental health needs of students, the researcher discussed with the teachers there. Findings are as follows:

- "Students remain with us only for four to five hours, rest they remain in the same environment which is not good. So, the efforts taken by the teachers for the child are not so effective."
- "Schools are in bad condition like there is double shifts system in most of the schools. So, the chances of getting the school property damaged become double and once it gets broken it will remain unrepaired till the next order (which comes from higher authority) for the repairing of furniture. Secondly, in rainy season, not only water comes in the class rooms, but all dirt and squalor of the slum flow in.
- "I lost all my knowledge after coming here and this has not only happened with me, but with many of us. Because when you join the job you are knowledgeable, as you clear the DSSB (Delhi Subordinate Service Selection) examination. But, after four five years you start getting

dumb because teaching here is not two way process, but is only one way monologue as others (students) are hopeless, then till how long you can stand in front of them. A day comes when you also become dumb and get depressed."

- "I am not enjoying teaching in Municipal Corporation of Delhi School. Here teachers have to bear an extra burden, meaning their main job is teaching, but here we have to do everything else, but proper teaching like distributing scholarship, money, uniforms, books, shoes, and preparing various bills. Secondly, if one has to take a leave, then they have to visit their office several times to get it sanctioned. Before getting this job I was in a private school where one has to take only classes and nothing beyond that, which really made me feel happy."
- "Department is not giving funds to the schools for celebrating any festival. These children never had attended good functions. They come in school dress on every occasion (if they have) and do something or other on the stage. There is nothing new and innovative for them as there are no resources so the routine remains dumb."
- "There is no charm in this job, you only have to come here and sit for five hours and go back to home on time. Only good thing in this job is that one has to work half day."
- "The condition of evening staff is miserable as there are very less officials visit in the evening. So, the teachers feel free at that time. Secondly, male staff is there, as they are bold by nature, so, they can handle the situation if anything happens against them".
- "A senior male teacher in my staff rarely takes classes and if anybody says anything then he starts howling and writes letters to the higher authorities about the loop-holes of the school which no doubt every school has so nobody says anything to him."—Said by one of the evening staff teacher.
- "There is no proper provision of basic facilities like proper black board, furniture; chalks etc. then how a teacher can work effectively in such conditions."

- "There in lots of jealousy in the staff members, even in case of small staff. We have a staff of ten teachers yet groups exist in our staff and to survive our-self we have to play tricks."
- "Being a Muslim area (East Delhi) schools remain empty at the time of *Namaz* and you cannot say anything to them as it is a religious matter."
- "Muslim community children also go to their Mosque to study Urdu. Which is no doubt a good thing, but they usually avoid their studies because of that and for this their parents give excuse that Urdu is more important to study than school education."

The above mentioned viewpoints and findings reflect the feelings of teachers about school management which shows frustration and apathy. According to the teachers, this is applicable to a majority of schools (approximately 70% of Municipal Corporation of Delhi Schools), and not a condition in their school only.

Perception of Parents about School Social Work

(i) With Social Work

To know the perception of the parents of Municipal School children, the researcher talked with eight parents (two from each school). The parents were unaware about the concept of social work. Six of them even did not know about the NGO working in their children's school. Only two of them said, "*haan, bachche batate to hain ki kuch bachchon ko alag madam padhati hain* (yes, children have told that to some kids, a different teacher teaches)". The other one also added "*jinko hindi ki kitab padhna nahi ata unko padhate hain* (those children who cannot read Hindi, are taught by special teachers)". For all of them, sending their wards to school is just to confine to become literate and getting pass in every class. They do not bother about marks and other developmental needs of their children. According to them, the children are first generation learners so they do whatever is instructed by the teacher as they (parents) do not know anything about education.

(ii) Without Social Work

The perceptions of these parents (eight parents—two from each) were also almost the same. They also shared the same sentiments that "*hum to ye chahte hain ki hamare bachche hum jaisse anpadh na rahe. Do char akshar jane to hum jesse dukhi na hon* (we just want that our children should not remain illiterate like us, if they learn something, they would not be miserable like us)". But when researcher asked the parents about their meetings with the teacher they said, "*dekho ji hum karte hai roj dihadi pe kam, agar roj chhutti lenge to khayenge kya*? (see, we are daily-wagers, if we take off [to attend PTM or meet teachers] what will we eat?)." Another parent said, "*humen khud kuch na ata hum kya baat karen* (we ourselves do not know anything, what will we talk?)." The researcher asked whether they were called by teachers or not, for this they said, "*bulate to hain par vahi baat hai aaye kaise*? (they do call, but we cannot come)". Below are the enlisted points, that emerged out of the discussions with parents of the students studying in Government Schools:

- Most parents are daily wagers and they cannot afford to come and meet the class teacher at the cost of their wages.
- These people are uneducated and hence cannot help their children in their studies.
- Economic hardship limits the provision of educational facilities to the children.

Being illiterate, they have no idea of the nuances of education process and so they blindly rely on what the teachers say. A school is a unique human institution it has certain aims and ideals to be achieved and for that it works with the available human and material resources which constitutes headmaster/principal, teachers, special staff (optional) and students. Harmonious interplay of these subsystems plays crucial role in fulfilling the objective of imparting education by the school otherwise any dysfunctional interaction between these members hampers the educational process.

Conclusion

This chapter has dealt with the situation in Government Schools with regard to social workers. Findings show that in real sense no school social worker is appointed in the Government Schools, where they are needed the most. The posts of "social workers" were created and appointments were made, but these professionals were neither from social work discipline nor did they take up any "social work" related activities. They were involved in teaching. Recently certain NGOs have been linked with Government Schools that facilitate children, especially, who are first generation learners, to cope with the pressure of studies. There is high scope and intense need of social workers, in view of psycho-social problems faced by students, but the Government has taken no initiative to appoint social workers in the schools.

References

Delhi Directorate of Education, New Delhi: Ministry of Education. Retrieved From https://en.wikipedia.org/wiki/Delhi_Directorate_of_Education

Municipal Corporation of Delhi (MCD). Retrieved from https://en.wikipedia.org/wiki/Municipal_Corporation_of_Delhi

5

Comparative Analysis of School Social Work in Private and Government Schools

School social workers have long been concerned about children who are not able to use what education has to offer. Over the span of a century, schools broadened their mission and scope towards becoming more inclusive and towards ensuring respect for the individual differences of all children. Consequently, social workers and many educators have come to share similar tasks and objectives. Each person possesses intrinsic worth. Schools and families are environments where children should develop, discover their own dignity and worth, and come to realize their potential. Unfortunately, the human potential of each person is often needlessly wasted due to dysfunctional family systems or apathetic school systems. School social workers work with children and their school and family environments, assisting them to accomplish tasks associated with their learning, growth, and development, and thus to come to a fuller realization of their intrinsic dignity, capability, and potential. The role of school social worker is developed from this purpose and these values. It is not simply doing clinical social work in a school.

The basic focus of the school social worker is the liaison between teachers, parents, and children. In the present study we came across four types of school systems and gathered information on relevance and applicability of school social work. Data have also been qualitatively reflected through cases that speak volumes on the vital role played by a social worker in school setting.

Unlike in most parts of the West, India does not have common school system. Class division is reflected in schooling system and we have schools run by private enterprises and also by the Government under its Constitutional obligation to provide social service to all its citizens. The Government and private schools differ in terms of building infrastructure and related facilities for educational and extra-curricular activities. Well-ventilated, spacious class-rooms, suitable and comfortable furniture, smart-boards, teaching aids, well equipped library and laboratories, computer rooms, playground, swimming pool, ultra-modern technological support system to facilitate teaching, and such others are the common characteristics of private schools in Delhi.

On the contrary, Government schools may or may not have buildings and sufficient classrooms, desks and chairs. Many of Government schools are still functional in temporary tents or tin-sheds. The Government schools definitely lack sufficient computers, smart-boards, and innovative facilities in teaching learning aids.

Staff shortage in terms of teachers and Para-teaching Staff is a feature of Government Schools while private schools do have ample human resource to ensure high quality of education and related facilities for their students. Private schools organize trips for their students to abroad as well as to different places in India. Every year, many private schools take their children to NASA (USA), Italy, Singapore etc. and in many places in India include wildlife sanctuary, historical monuments, and such others to provide exposure to their students. In Government schools, such exposure visits are organized at places where teachers are comfortable in taking the students. Trip to abroad are almost non-existent in Government Schools.

For admitting and making their wards study in private schools, parents have to shell out ample money as school fees while in Government Schools either education is free of cost or minimal charges are taken from students.

The profile of children studying in these schools may be looked into. The students coming to private schools largely hail from middle, upper middle class and rich families. The parents know the value of education and make their best of efforts to ensure that their offsprings get quality education. The parents have intention as well as resources to meet the financial requirements of private schools, where their children are studying. However, with recent Right to Education Act, 2012, 25 per cent seats are reserved for children from Economically Weaker Sections (EWS). This move has changed the composition of students in a classroom in a private school. And it has also posed challenges for the school authorities to adjust to the changing demands of emerging scenario.

In contrast, the children in Government Schools are, more or less, from families having economic constraints. The parents of these children are largely illiterate or semi-literate engaged in semi-skilled jobs and hard-pressed of money. They lack enough resources to match the expenditure on education with the parents whose children are in private schools.

In this backdrop, let us first analyze the roles and activities performed by social workers in private schools. In the study, the researcher could not locate social workers in most of the private schools. The schools having social workers do have an edge over those not having social workers. Broadly, social workers perform their tasks under the following categories:

1. Handling cases of children having behavioural problems.
2. Inclusive Education.
3. SUPW.

Handling Cases of Children having Behavioural Problems

The task of school social worker that is chiefly related to his/her professional expertise in dealing with cases of children having any problems manifested in their behaviours and resulting in their reduced capacity to take in fruits of education. There is wide range of factors that may result in problems among children—high parental expectations may put pressure among children resulting in performance anxiety. Every year, during results time, newspapers are full of news items about suicides and suicidal attempts by students for not being able to score marks as per the expectations of teachers and parents. Childhood is no longer a time characterized by care-free and rejoices. Examination anxiety is becoming a common reality. Then, families may undergo social, emotional and financial crisis and marital conflicts, domestic violence, abuses and exploitation by one family member on the other is becoming common. This disrupts the psychological well-being of the child and his/her studies. Parenting styles (authoritarian or permissive) too impact the child and may result into behavioural problems. The social worker deals with children approaching to him/her with any of these problems.

Psychologists have maintained that most of the psychological problems, whether minor or serious mental illnesses have their roots in childhood. Invariably, children having any behavioural issues too have causal roots in their families. Social worker is an expert having skills and knowledge to rectify the problems. He/she is a biggest resource for a school and his/her interventions have the potential to not only solve the affected child's problems there and then, but also curbing its effects reaching to adulthood. In the study, in private schools, social workers have resolved conflicts from the lives of numerous pupils each year. This preventive intervention is highly cost-effective.

However, the public schools as well as government schools not having social workers, rely on their teachers to perform this role of social worker. However, since 'helping' the children in need is not the primary duty of a teacher and he/she is paid for teaching and not counselling the child, often times, in private schools, a teacher wears the hat of a social worker or counsellor only and when she/he has free time and/or inclination. Since, a teacher is not duty bound to 'counsel' the child facing behavioural/emotional problems, he/she cannot be held accountable for not doing so. Thus, in private schools without social workers, the highly significant service of dealing with emotional and behavioural problems of a child takes a back seat.

However, the study brings an interesting finding. Most of the private schools without social workers, appoint a counsellor to handle children having adjustment and behavioural problems. It is the perception of many teachers and principals from the schools that are not having social workers that a counsellor can easily take-up the role of a social worker. Although both of them may provide intervention, advocacy, referrals to outside agencies for further assistance, there is difference in the impact of their work.

Let us analyze the difference between the services offered by a counsellor and those by a social worker in the school setting.

School Social Workers	*Counsellors*
School Social workers work on improving the functional relations between the child, school, family (parents) and community.	Counsellors are concerned with intra-psychic issues and are not much concerned with intervention in social environment.
They follow ecological approach.	They follow psycho-analytical or Cognitive Behaviour approaches.
They hold the Master's degree in social work.	They hold Master's degree in psychology or counselling.
Cases dealt by social worker are of wide range: from financial troubles to relationship concerns, children with special needs and mental health issues.	Cases dealt by counsellors are generally related to slow learners, behavioural problems, academic deterioration etc.
Social workers also work on creating empathy, citizenship conscience; rights based approach, social justice and equality.	Counsellors generally focus on the academic growth and achievements, for example providing career guidance.
They expose the students to harsh realities of life such as poverty, abuse, marginalization etc and make them well equipped to 'help' the downtrodden.	They counsel the child and parents for betterment of child.
School social work is a specialized area and students of social work are exposed to practical training so that when they are in job, they are well-equipped to perform their roles.	Counsellors are also master level professionally trained in psychology. They invariably do not have field-exposure while doing masters.

This apart, findings in the study show that though counsellors are present in most private schools in place of social workers, they are not proactive. While many times, social workers themselves locate children having problems, counsellors do not do so. The interviews with students have clearly reflected that they were hardly satisfied with the services of a counsellor as compared to students of the schools having social workers, where satisfaction levels were very high. This gives strong justification for having social workers in the schools.

Since, in most situations where there are no social worker in schools, teachers take-up the role of handling children having behavioural problems. The table below differentiates the services of handling behavioural problems provided by a teacher in contrast to a social worker in the school setting.

Difference between Teacher and Social Worker

School Social Workers	*Teachers*
They have necessary knowledge and skills to handle people facing problems, through their training in social work.	Teachers invariably lack sufficient expertise to deal with children facing familial dysfunctioning and/or domestic violence.
In the study, students were satisfied with their school social worker and consider her approachable, expert and considerate.	In the study, students consider their teachers ill-equipped to handle their emotional problems. They were rude and full of moral preaching.
Students reported that social workers maintained strict confidentiality in their cases, which they felt has enhanced their confidence on her.	Students informed that teachers largely were biased and prejudiced, and told everyone in the school about their problems.
Social workers have designated time to resolve conflicts faced by children as they are full time appointed for this task, among other related activities.	Teachers are overburdened with finishing their syllabus, checking notebooks, preparing assignments, question papers etc. They lack time. The teachers in government schools are entrusted with additional tasks such as disbursing scholarship, books, stationary, arranging for mid-day meals etc.
Social workers are appointed for handling cases of pupils' problems and they have time and space for this duty.	For teachers, handling cases of children with problems is not the part of their jobs and they do so in free time.
Dealing with problems of students is the part of their job profile and they are accountable for it.	Teachers are not accountable to resolve students' behavioural problems. Teachers in Government Schools refrain from involving themselves in handling cases of children due to threats given by rowdy boys.
Social workers have scientific and technical know-how of dealing with problems like alcoholism, aggression, violence, infatuation etc., commonly found among school children.	Teachers do not possess that knowledge as a part of their training.

Findings from the interviews of students clearly reflect that teachers, more often than not, do not understand the psyche of the student community and enforce their moral values on them. They are often judgemental and prejudiced. Case studies mentioned above also validate these findings.

Thus, schools need a full time social worker who has the necessary skills and expertise to handle wide range of problems faced by students. This task cannot be left to teachers who often do not have time and/or inclination and definitely do not have expertise.

Inclusive Education

The second most prominent task of a social worker is integration and inclusion of children with disabilities with the 'mainstream' class. Findings have clearly shown that in selected few schools where social workers are appointed, inclusive education is a reality while in other private schools either there is separate unit for special children or they avoid admitting children with disabilities. A few parents validated that certain schools come up with many excuses while asking to give admission to their disabled child. In Government Schools, under Universalisation of Elementary Education and Sarva Shiksha Abhiyan, there are special educators for children with disabilities. However, they are not stationed in one school and entrusted with the responsibilities of many schools. So, they do not have time to provide to a differently abled child, helping him/her adjust and integrate in the 'normal' classroom. Government schools have huge number of children with learning and other disabilities and scope of social work is vast. In reality, no efforts are done to meet the demands.

Certain schools where social workers are appointed, each and every child with special needs is given sufficient time, handholding is done by the social worker herself to integrate him/her in the normal class. For about a month, a mentor or social worker or trainee social worker sits with the child with special needs in the mainstream class. Schools without social workers do not have manpower to provide individualized services to children with special needs. So, they avoid admitting children with disabilities in their schools or have special unit where no effort for integration is made.

Thus, social workers are well-equipped to facilitate inclusion of children with disabilities in the mainstream education. However, in most private and government schools, no other staff (teacher or counsellor or special educator) has been able to substitute the role of social worker.

SUPW Related Activities

SUPW and community service are the other crucial activities performed by school social workers. The aim of these activities is to conscientize the school children towards the needs of their poor and marginalized counterparts and to create a sense of "service to the society" and brotherhood. These services also help the children to develop values like social justice and rights-based approach. In the globalized world, these exposures help the children remain grounded and develop civic responsibilities. When children observe that many families in slums and resettlement colonies struggle hard to earn meals for survival, they learn to appreciate what they have and share their resources with the disadvantaged fellow-beings. Such experiences inculcate maturity, empathy and sensitivity. Social workers play crucial role in these exposures. In Government Schools, no community work is done and reportedly, all decisions are taken by the Government and orders are passed by the Education Department. Students from schools having social workers informed how they have changed and how good they feel after helping their fellow beings in slum areas. Such responses were not therefrom students of private schools without social workers.

Thus, school social workers play significant role in making students conscientize and well aware, sensitive citizens geared towards helping their poor and marginalized fellow-beings. The schools without social workers are at much loss as none is working on inculcating values of responsible citizenry among their students.

Except these, there are few other works which come under the purview of school social worker and a teacher cannot do them as they are not accountable. The roles are discussed below:

Organize Income Generation Programme

Income Generating programmes are meant for the community

people or for the physically and mentally challenged people like candle making, providing the needy people computer training, beauty culture, stitching classes etc. The motto of this was to provide these people a skill so that they can become economically self-reliant.

Layouts for New Projects

Social workers make layouts for the new projects. For this, they make a report under the following heads:

- Name of Project.
- Why the Project should be Launched.
- Aim of the Project.
- Who are the Parts of the Project?
- Target Group.
- Duration.
- Resources Needed.
- Expenditure on the Project etc.

After making layout the social worker consults it with the Principal and finalizes the report. Then, she executes the project after getting approval from the principal.

Liaison with Outside Agencies

School social workers liaison with outside agencies for various reasons like for referring cases, for fund raising or for collaborating on different projects, for expert advice etc. It is very much important for the worker to be in touch with various organizations working in diverse fields of social work. Secondly, liaison also makes the social worker resourceful and keeps her updated on various social issues. The more resourceful the social worker is the more successful she is in her work.

Organizing Camps

School social workers organize camps time to time on various social issues like health, education, sanitation etc. They are organized not only to create awareness among the community people, but also to develop a sense of responsibility among the students who participate in the camps. Involving the students is to make them understand about the matter/issue thoroughly and as the children are future nation builders, so making them aware is important so that they will create awareness among others.

Adoption of a Community

Schools with social workers can adopt one or two communities, nearby their school with the motto "either take school to the community or bring community to the school". Because schools are the inseparable part of community so it is important that both move simultaneously. The school can run different projects in their respective communities, like literacy, awareness, vocational training, counselling services etc. For this they can involve their students in doing various works. The motto of adopting the slum area is that children realize the manifestation of impoverishment and there is a lot of scope to work to ameliorate the conditions of slum dwellers. This not only boosts the confidence level of school children, but also makes them aware of social realities and develops feeling of brotherhood and compassion.

Briefing and Sensitizing the Staff About their Activities

It is very important work because if a teacher is aware of the various activities of school social work then it will be easier for them to cooperate with school social worker and participate and contribute to the programmes running in the school under the gamut of social work unit. Secondly, it is helpful for creating better understanding between teachers and the school social workers.

Social workers, in the study, maintained that it is important to orient and sensitize teachers about our programmes so that their cooperation can be sought. Sensitization is needed from lower level to higher level like from grade IV to the level of Principal. Sensitization sessions involve each and every member of the school.

Handling various Social Welfare Projects

All social welfare projects come under the purview of school social worker, so for this the social worker has to do each and every work like making blue print of projects, estimation of manpower required when the project starts, planning and execution of the project. Apart from this, supervising and evaluating the project are also the part of the social worker's responsibilities. The social worker is the one who looks after the progress of every social welfare project.

Preparation for Awards

To enhance prestige and credibility of the school, the social worker has to make various reports and submit them for different awards at the inter-school levels or state or national levels. This work not only brings pride to the school, but also provides good recognition to the work of social worker.

Fund Raising

The school social workers raise funds for various purposes like for helping the children from economically weaker section or starting any new project (in case the school provides less money for the same). Under fund raising programmes, various range of resources are tapped from local sources such as cash, clothes, medicines, old books of students to be given to the needy ones. Social workers also motivate children to make best out of waste materials so that they also learn to conserve environment by recycling and reusing goods. These materials are then sold and money collected is utilized for the proposed activities. Students raise resources for any calamities faced by people anywhere in the country, and the collected materials are handed over to the needy people through some NGOs or individually by the school.

The social workers not only raise the funds, but also maintain records of it so that transparency can be maintained. All work is done with the permission of Principal. The way of raising funds totally depends on the skills and ability of every school social worker, and everyone adopts different ways and modalities for this.

Conclusion

This chapter was based on the comparative analysis to private and government schools, both with and without social workers. In private schools with social workers the students and teachers were highly satisfied with the roles and responsibilities of social workers. In private schools without social workers, the teachers, sporadically, tend to take up role of social workers, but lack the prerequisite values and skills. In government schools, a handful of teachers carry the designation of social workers, but do not take up any tasks in situation to social work. Certain government schools are linked with NGOs and helping the weaker children in the studies. The next chapter concludes the major findings of the study and provides suggestions.

6
Summary and Suggestions

Social work has ample scope in education settings. School social workers are one of the many professionals who facilitate the education process so that the students gain maximum benefits from their schooling. As professionals working closely with children and their families, social workers play a valuable role in ensuring children's well-being. For over a century, school social workers have been providing a critical link between school, home and community. These professionals in school settings, have consistently focused on coordinating the efforts of schools, families and communities towards helping students improve their academic achievements and social, emotional and behavioural competence. Social workers use their unique perspective of viewing the person in his or her social environment (systems approach) and intervene to improve the social functioning of the children.

The schools are places where children acquire education. However, this social institution is not free of stressors and factors that create and perpetuate inequality, frustration, anxiety, misery and sufferings among the children. In the school system social workers come across wide range of problems such as bullying, aggression, violence, caste and gender-based discrimination, alcoholism, drug addiction, infatuations, love betrayals, emotional upsurges, depression, anxiety, inferiority-superiority, health issues, differential mental and learning capabilities and heightened parental expectations for academic excellence, emotional and social maladjustments arising out of children coming from families in conflict or broken families, physical, mental and social disabilities. School social workers handle these cases as part of their job profile.

Literature review brought out that school social work is a vital component of most of the schools in the Western countries and social workers play crucial role in ensuring mental health and social well-being of children in the education settings. However, in India, it is still in its nascent stage. School social work has received meagre research attention in the Indian settings.

In this backdrop, the present study was conceptualized with the aim to document and examine the tasks performed by school social workers in private and Government Schools. The study also looks into those schools (private as well as Government) not having social workers and analyzes the differences in the schools in terms of tasks involved in facilitating teaching-learning environment.

The study is located in Delhi. It has adopted Descriptive Research Design with qualitative approach. Using stratified random sampling, three types of schools were taken-up—private schools (thirty two), Delhi Government Schools (thirty-two) and Municipal Corporation Schools (sixteen). Out of which (eight) private schools, (eight) Delhi Government Primary Schools and (four) Municipal Corporation Schools were taken from each zone. In the second layer of stratification, each type of school has been divided on the basis of presence or absence of social workers. So, out of eight private schools, four with social workers and four without social workers were covered in the study. Similarly, four Government Schools with social workers and four without social workers were included in the study. Two Municipal Schools with school social work and two without social worker were included in the study. Interviews were done with school social workers in private and Government schools to document their roles and tasks. Alongside, the Principals, two teachers, five students and two parents with social workers from schools and those without social workers were interviewed.

Thematic analysis of the findings was done.

Findings

All the schools do not have social workers. Schools having social workers are mainly in south and west zones of Delhi. Eight private schools having social workers were covered in the study. There is no clear cut role demarcation in relation to designation. Social workers and counsellors share role ambiguity *vis-à-vis* their designation. While many private schools have counsellors and their role is confined to providing career counselling and guidance only, in one of the sampled school the professional with the designation 'counsellor' was performing the tasks of social worker.

Only one social worker, in the study, has M.A. Social Work degree, others were mainly post-graduates in Psychology or Education. Apart from role and designation ambiguity, even professionals from other disciplines like Psychology and Education have been appointed as school social workers.

All social workers in the study were females. Female professionals prefer jobs as school social workers, may be because of ease in striking balance between family and career. They were getting grade pay of a TGT or PGT depending upon their years of service. There was no uniform practice across the schools in terms of work timings and work profile of social workers. Usually, they have to stay for extra 2-3 hours above school timings.

In many private schools, counsellors are appointed who focus only on career counselling. Social workers in school settings perform whole range of tasks and activities, along with holding sessions on career counselling occasionally.

There is high variability in models of school social work in the Government Schools and none is found effective. Most Government schools do not have social workers. Directorate of Education in 1980s appointed 131 "social workers" under their Adult Education Programme. The appointees were either war widows or diploma holders from ITI. Their job was to take nursery classes and adult education classes. In December 2004, the project was closed and all the appointed social workers were sent to Sarvodaya Vidyalayas. In these schools, they take classes or do administrative work, as per the directions of the Principals. Their posts would dissolve with their retirement. Here, only designation of appointees is "social worker" while their work profile is nowhere related to school social workers, as we understand in common parlance.

In addition, there are special educators under Universal Elementary Education (UEE) project who are entrusted with the responsibilities of handling children with special needs in Government Schools. However, each special educator is given six schools to cover.

This apart, in many feeder schools of Delhi Government, NGOs are collaborating and holding certain programmes for children within the school premises.

Thus, different models of school social work are operational in Government and private schools and there is high elusiveness and indistinctness with regard to designation and work profile of social workers in these two types of educational institutions.

The variability is also observed in the job profile of social workers across the schools. Social workers, in private schools, are performing varied roles like case work with children having problems, community work, and inclusive education with differently abled children, SUPW and educational enrichment programmes. Though private schools without social workers and Government schools (with and without social workers) claim to take-up some of these roles, their effectiveness is under question.

Case work with children or helping individual children facing any problems that are hampering their studies are taken-up and resolved by school social workers. Social workers annually handle 6-7 major, long-term and complex cases while cases with not so serious problems are numerous. Meetings with parents are held and home visits are paid, whenever required.

In private schools, teachers claim to handle children having problems. However, without training and required knowledge, their expertise is under question. Also, work overload (taking classes, checking notebooks, assignments, making question papers, checking answer scripts etc.) may not leave them with 'free time' to take-up additional responsibility. In addition, teachers are not held accountable if they do not intervene in children's problems. This makes teachers an ineffective substitution of school social worker.

In Government schools, particularly in girls' shift, many teachers find themselves capable of handling problems of children, but actual helping is related to particular teacher's inclination and 'free time'. If a teacher decides to ignore the problems, nothing can be done. In boys' shift, due to indiscipline and rowdiness of many "anti-social" boys, teachers refrain from involving themselves in issues and problems of the students of their class.

In pre-primary schools of the Government, where the need of social work professional is most necessary as children coming from nearby resettlement colonies and slum areas, face multiple social, emotional and financial vulnerabilities, teachers are overburdened with responsibilities such as disbursement of scholarship, books, shoes, uniform, stationary, arranging for mid-day meals, filling-up Ladli forms and such others, along with teaching.

A high level of frustration was observed among teachers of Government Schools as they are burdened with responsibilities of disbursement of items under various social welfare schemes, having little scope to teach. Moreover, their efforts in teaching are not valued and recognized. School administration and parents are unconcerned about the quality of education. Children are too young to understand anything (in Municipal Schools) or too smart to threaten teachers if they resist their wrong-doings (in higher secondary schools). A frustrated teacher cannot handle problems of children or even encourage them to do well in academics.

Thus, lack of technical expertise, work pressure, unwillingness, are some factors that raise doubts over teachers replacing social workers.

School students found social workers most approachable and suitable to resolve their problems. In schools without social workers, where teachers are handling pupils' problems, level of satisfaction is lowest. Students found their teachers lacking maturity, breaking confidentiality and having stereotypes and prejudices as far as handling their problems was concerned.

Inclusive education is another major role taken-up by school social workers. In schools having social workers, a well-organized system is in place where at the entry level a disabled child is in special wing/unit and gradually included in the mainstream class. Social workers, either themselves or in their close supervision through trainees or student-mentors, do hand-holding of the child with special needs in making him/her adjust in the mainstream class.

Some of the private schools, without social workers, do not have special units for children with disabilities and they hardly do attempts to integrate children with special needs into mainstream classes. Most other private schools make excuses and abstain from admitting children with disabilities.

As a matter of policy, Government Schools cannot afford to deny admission to children with disabilities. In fact, in Government Schools, as per the version of teachers, more than a half of the children have learning or the other kind of disabilities. Government has appointed special educators, but each one has six schools under his/her jurisdiction. A child with special needs does not get enough time and support from the special educators so as to overcome his/her disability in contrast to private schools having social workers who have dexterity as well as time and patience to move at the pace of the child having disabilities and gradually make him/her adjust in the mainstream class.

Thus, the role of a social worker in ensuring inclusive education for children with special needs is vital and irreplaceable.

Another significant role of school social workers is the community work. The aim of this is to inculcate values of social justice, human rights, empathy, compassion and responsible citizenry among the students. When the students of private schools (who invariably belong to economically well off families) visit slum areas and meet people there, they observe sufferings and pains for the first time. This exposure makes them sensitive and empathetic. When students teach illiterate poor inhabitants of slum areas, they learn sense of purpose, responsibility towards fellow-beings, social justice and rights-based approach. In addition, children learn to divert their attention and energy in positive and creative direction.

Private schools without social workers do not generally have component of community work. Children and adolescents in such schools do not have opportunity to channelize their energy unlike their counterparts studying in schools where social workers engage them in community work.

Students gave positive feedback about their work in the communities. They are happy to help their needy fellow-beings and are proud of themselves for taking up such work. However, parents of schools having social work, at times, face programmatic challenges such as picking their wards much later after school hours, and hence do not appreciate proactive engagement of "social work" by the school. Many parents and teachers from private schools do not recognize the values learnt by students through community work and believe that ultimately academic excellence of the student would prove beneficial and not the community work. However, more than two-thirds of parents and teachers informed that children are learning values that would make them good human being, which is very important and now-a-days, families are failing to inculcate such values.

In Government Schools, no long-term engagement with nearby deprived communities are done, though sporadically awareness campaigns (say on sanitation, public health etc.) are organized.

For inculcating social responsibility, schools are required to have credited component called "Socially Useful and Productive Work" (SUPW). In schools with social workers, the responsibilities of conducting activities related to SUPW are entrusted with school social workers. There are activities within the school such as plantation, making best out of waste, environmental conservation, mentoring disabled children and such others.

In private schools without social workers, SUPW activities are done as credits are associated with it. However, activities are, more often than not, planned and executed sporadically and often done in mundane manner. Same is the case with Government schools.

Many pre-primary schools are attached with NGOs who provide support in terms of teaching aids, books, remedial classes and such others. However, since the NGO functionaries are not the part of the school system (in contrast to the model where social workers in private schools are the part of the school system), they do not have much flexibility and authority to make changes for the betterment of children.

Principals of private schools without social workers are of the belief that teachers are the best persons for resolving the conflicts of their students and no social workers are required. Career counselling is done by the part-time and full-time appointed counsellors.

Principals of Government Schools do recognize the relevance of social workers, but do not have authority to appoint them on their own. All decisions regarding creating or dissolving posts rest with the Government policy-makers.

Principals of schools having social workers have realized the relevance of social workers and have appointed them in their respective schools.

School social work is the need of the hour, having potential to rectify most of the problems faced by the pupils, with root cause either at the family level or in the school. Social workers have, beyond doubt, proven their worth and capacities by regaining mental well-being and rectifying social relations with significant others through their intervention. The schools where social workers are not appointed lack certain systems and practices to recognize the mental health needs of the children, to address their problems and respond to their crises effectively. And, specialized services offered by social workers cannot be substituted by any other professionals like teachers, special educators and career counsellors.

Suggestions

In the light of the above findings, following suggestions are offered:

1. Social workers are very much required in all the schools. The policy-level recommendation is made to appoint social workers in all the schools, whether private or government.
2. Since, social work education provides requisite knowledge and skills to deal with crisis situations people face and ameliorate the sufferings of the individuals, groups and communities, appointment of social workers having Master's degree in social work should be made mandatory.
3. Designation and role clarity should be specific *vis-à-vis* social workers in the school settings. In long-run, that would carve a space for social workers in different institutions including schools. Then, as with most other professions, designation signifies role specifications (for instance, Surgeon, Engineer, Chartered Accountant etc.), the same would happen with social work profession.
4. Social work educational institutions should place students

for their concurrent placements in various schools, Government as well as private, so that the school authorities realize the relevance of social work in educational setting. In India, social work began with certain colleges of social work such as Nirmala Niketan, started sending their trainees in schools. Revival of such a trend would lead to expansion of social work in school settings as well as would be a very beneficial service for the students.

5. Sensitization through exposure, discussions of Principals and school authorities of private schools about the nuances of social work may expand school social work in all the private schools.
6. Social activists and advocates working for the betterment of education system should be made to realize the potential role of social workers in the schools so that required policy level initiatives can be taken-up.
7. In Government Schools, social workers may play crucial role in ensuring quality education and reducing dropout rates. The study has depicted ample scope of social work in Government Schools, starting from feeder schools to higher secondary schools. Mandatory appointment of social workers in Government schools would be a welcome step that has the capacity to drastically improve educational scenario.
8. School social workers may focus on preventive services to deal with stress, aggression, violence, examination anxiety, problems related to adolescent phase, drug abuse and such others, which would be cost effective in the long-run.
9. At times, teachers too are stressed out and frustrated due to personal reasons or factors present in the workplace. Social workers can expand their services of counselling to teachers too. That would ensure mental well-being of teachers and enhance their teaching dexterity.
10. NGOs collaborating with pre-primary Government schools have high potential to work on many pressing issues and problems. This model, if led by social workers, can do

wonders in improving education system significantly.

11. Research work needs to be done on interventions done by social workers in school settings and documentation of best practices may be done and propagated and replicated.

Finally, it may be stated that school social work has a great potential to make the school system conducive for all the children, and make the education process more meaningful. It has the capacity to realize the Right to Education (and quality education) for all. Hopefully, the social planners and policy-makers soon recognize the value of school social work and make provisions to ensure their presence in each and every school of the country.

Conclusion

In this final chapter, an overview of the entire research, findings and analysis is provided. Significance of school social work is briefly mentioned. Objectives and research methodology are given in the snapshot. Summary, of findings are presented. Suggestions, in the light of major findings are offered. The research study observes the vital role played by the social workers in some schools and highly recommends that all the government and private schools must have social workers so that Right to Education to all the children-citizens is realized in its true sence.

Appendix

Interview Guide

Principal (With Social Work)

- Experience as Principal in the school.
- Knowledge of school social work.
- Roles and responsibilities of school social work.
- Benefits the school is getting from school social work.
- Facilities provided to the school social work.
- Integrated scheme of education.
- Need of school social work.
- Relation of school social worker with other staff members.
- Whom the social workers have to report.
- Opinion about school social worker and their work.

Principal (Without Social Work)

- Substitution of school social worker.
- Problems faced due to not having school social worker.
- School social worker should be a part of school or not.

Social Worker

- Job Profile.
- Experience in this field.
- Roles and responsibilities.
- Community involvement.
- Role in staff and parent meeting.
- Case studies.

- Record maintaining.
- Integrated school of education.
- Support from higher authorities.
- Acceptance among staff members.
- Adoption of any community.
- Projects going on.
- Mental health need of students and teachers.
- laison of school, home and community.
- Job satisfaction.
- Role perceived by them in near future.
- Scope of improvement.

Parents

- Awareness about school social work.
- Benefits of school social workers.
- Meetings with school social worker.
- Should be a part of school or not.

Teacher

- Awareness of school social work.
- Need of school social worker.
- Are school social workers working as helping hands?
- Role with staff members.
- They should be a part of school system or not.

Students

- Awareness about school social work.
- Need of school social work.
- Are they satisfied with the service?
- They should be the part of school system.

Bibliography

Books

Adolescent Education Programme (AEP), (2005), Ministry of HRD, Government of India, New Delhi: www.education.nic.in

Alderson, J.J. (1972), Models of School Social Work Practice. In R. Sarri & F. Maple (Eds.), *The School in the Community*. Washington, DC: National Association of Social Workers.

Allen-Meares, Paula (ed.) (2015), *Social Work Services in Schools*. 7th ed. New York: Pearson, Allyn, & Bacon.

Areson, C.W. (1923), *Status of Children's Work in the United States. Proceedings of the National Conference on Social Work*. Chicago: University of Chicago Press.

Barnard, W.M. (2004), Parent Involvement in Elementary School and Educational Attainment. *Children and Youth Services Review*, 26.

Bowen, N. (1999, January), A Role for School Social Workers in Promoting Student Success through School Family Partnership. *Social Work in Education,* Vol. 21, No.1.

Bowen, N. and Bowen, G.L. (1998, October), The Effect of Home Microsystem Risk Factors and School Microsystem, on Student Academic Performance and Effective Investment in Schooling. *Social Work in Education,* Vol. 20, No. 4.

Bowers, Swithun (1952), "The Nature and Definition of Social Case Work", *Principles and Techniques in Social Case Work* (ed.) Cora Kasius, New York.

Chavkin, Nancy Feyl. (1993), *The Use of Research in Social Work Practice: A Case Example from School Social Work*. Westport, CT: Praeger.

Constable, Robert T., Carol Rippey Massat, Shirley McDonald and John P. Flynn (2008), *School Social Work: Practice, Policy, and Research*, 7th ed. Chicago, IL: Lyceum.

Cook, Phillip J., Denise C. Gottfredson and Chongmin Na (2010), School Crime Control and Prevention, In *Crime and Justice: A Review of Research*, Vol. 39. Edited by Michael Tonry, 1–150. Chicago: Chicago Press.

Costin, L.B. (1978), *Social Work Services in School: Historical Perspective and Current Directions*, Continuing Education Series #8, Washington, D.C: National Association of Social Works.

Counts, George S. (1932), *Dare the School Build a New Social Order?* Carbondale, IL: Southern Illinois University Press.

Crosnoe, R., Johnson, M.K. and Elder, G.H. (2004), School Size and the Interpersonal side of Education: An Examination of Race/Ethnicity and Organizational Context. *Social Science Quarterly*, 85(5).

D'Souza, C., Syed. R., Sonaya, S. (1965), *Social Work Forum*, Vol. 3, No. 2.

Denaull, L. (1978 B), "Title T of ESEA: Utilizing the Social Work Service" in *Federal Legislation and the School Social Worker*, Washington, DC: National Association of Social Workers.

Domitrovich, Celene E., Catherine P. Bradshaw, Jeanne M. Poduska, *et al.* (2008), Maximizing the Implementation Quality of Evidence-based Preventive Interventions in Schools: *A Conceptual Framework. Advances in School Mental Health Promotion.*

Franklin, C. (2004), The Delivery of School Social Work Services. In P.A. Meares (Ed.), *Social Work Services in the School* (4th ed.), Boston, MA: Allyn & Bacon.

Franklin, Cynthia, Mary Beth Harris, and Paula Allen-Meares, (eds.) (2012). *The School Services Source Book: A Guide for School-based Professionals*. (2nd ed.) New York, NY: Oxford University Press.

Fredricksen, H. (1948), *The Child and His Welfare*. California: W.H. Freeman & Company, University of California.

Friedlander, W.A. (1963), *Introduction to Social Welfare*, New Delhi: Prentice Hall of India Pvt. Ltd.

G. A. Russell (1994), The Impact of the Philosophus Autodidactus: Pocockes, John Locke and the Society of Friends, in: G.A. Russell (ed.), *The 'Arabick' Interest of the Natural Philosophers in Seventeenth Century England,* Brill, Publishers, ISBN 90-04-09459-8.

Gandhi, A. (1990), *School Social Work*, New Delhi: Commonwealth Publishers.

Henderson, A. and Berla, N. (1994), A *New Generation of Evidence: The Family is Critical to Student Achievement*, Columbia, MD: National Committee for Citizens in Education.

Hendren, R., Birell Weisen, J. and Orley, J. (1994), *Mental Health Programmes in Schools*, Geneva: Division of Mental Health, WHO.

Hussain, Ch. Abid (June 2006), Effect of Guidance Services on Study Attitudes, Study Habits and Academic Achievement of Secondary School Students, *Bulletin of Education and Research*, Vol. 28, No. 1.

Institute of Medicine (1989), *Children and Adolescents with Mental, Behavioural and Development Disorders: Mobilizing a National Research Initiative*, Washington DC: National Academy of Sciences.

Joshi, S. (1996), *Child Survival, Health and Social Work Intervention*. New Delhi: Concept Publicing Company.

Kelly, Michael S. (2008), *The Domains and Demands of School Social Work Practice: A Guide to Working Effectively with Students, Families, and Schools*, New York: Oxford University Press.

MacMillan, K. (1980), *The Education Welfare Officer: Past, Present, and Future, Linking Home and School*, M. Craft, J. Raynor and L. Cohen, London: Harper & Row.

Mintzies, P.M. (1978), *The Emergency School Aid Act: Implications for Social Work Practices*. Washington DC: National Association of Social Workers.

National Mental Health Programme. (1982), New Delhi: Ministry of Health and Family Welfare, Government of India.

National Policy on Education (1986), New Delhi: Ministry of Human Resource Development, Department of Education, Government of India.

Openshaw, Linda (2008), *Social Work in Schools: Principles and Practice*, New York: Guilford.

Panda, A.K. (2005), *Elderly Women in Mega Polish*, New Delhi: Concept Publishing Company.

Peck, R.F. and Mitchell, J.V. (1962), *What Research Says to the Teacher Mental Health*, Washington DC: American Educational Research Association.

Robinson, M. (1978), *School and Social Work*, London: Routledge & Kegan Paul.

Sikkema, M. (1951), "School Social Work Services", *Social Work Yearbook*, Margaret, E.H., (Ed.), New York: American Association of Social Workers.

Stuart, M. (1970), *One Hundred Years of London Education; 1870-1970*, Allen Lane. London: The Penguin Press.

The Education Act, 1944, (1944), London: HMSO.

Thyer, Bruce A., and Laura L. Myers. (2007), *A Social Worker's Guide to Evaluating Practice Outcomes*, Alexandria, VA: Council on Social Work Education.

Ting, L., Jacobson, J.M. and Sanders, S. (2008), "Available Supports and Coping Behaviours of Mental Health Social Workers Following Fatal and Non-fatal Client Suicidal Behaviour," *Social Work*, 53(3).

Trecker, H.B. (1955), *Social Group Work: Principles and Practices*. New York: Association Press.

Walberg, H.J. (1981), A Psychological Theory of Educational Productivity. In F.H. Farley & N.U. Gordon (Eds.), *Psychology and Education*. Berkeley, CA: McCutchan.

Weatherly, R. (1978), *The Education for all Handicapped Children Act of 1975*, Washington, DC: National Association of Social Workers.

WHO (1996), *Life Skill Education in Schools*, Geneva: Division of Mental Health, WHO.

Journals

Agarwal, R. and Kapoor, M. (1998), Parent's Participation in Children academic activities in relation to their academic achievement at the primary level, *Journal of Indian Education*, Vol. XXIII (4).

Allen-Meares, P. (2006), One Hundred Years: A Historical Analysis of Social Work Services in Schools. *School Social Work Journal*, Special Issue, 24-43.

Appelbaum and Chambliss, (1997), Cited in Article, Power and Conformity in Today's Schools, Justin Saldana, Ph.D., published in *International Journal of Humanities and Social Science*, Vol. 3, No. 1; January 2013.

Banerjee, G.R. (1965), "School Social Services: Its Potentialities", *The Indian Journal of Social Work*, Vol. 26, No. 3.

Battle, J. and Lewis, M. (2002), The Increasing Significance of Class: The Relative Effects of Race and Socio-economic Status on Academic Achievement, *Journal of Poverty, 6(2).*

Frey, Andy J. and David R. Dupper (2005), A Broader Conceptual Approach to Clinical Practice for the 21st Century, *Children and Schools Journals*, Washington DC: National Association of Social Workers, NASW Press.

Henslin (1999), Cited in Article, Power and Conformity in Today's Schools, Justin Saldana, Ph.D., published in *International Journal of Humanities and Social Science,* Vol. 3, No. 1. January 2013.

Hussain, Ch. Abid (June 2006), Effect of Guidance Services on Study Attitudes, Study Habits and Academic Achievement of Secondary School Students. *Bulletin of Education and Research,* Vol. 28, No. 1 (35-45), 10.

Leyba, E.G. (2009), Tools to Reduce Overload in the School Social Worker Role, *Children & Schools Journals*, Washington, DC: National Association of Social Workers, NASW Press.

Pistorius, K.D., Feinauer, L.L., Harper, J.M., Stabmann, R.F. and Miller, R.B. (2008), Working with sexually abused children. *The American Journal of Family Therapy,* 36.

Saldana, Justin (2013), Power and Conformity in Today's Schools, *International Journal of Humanities and Social Sciences,* Vol. 3, No. 1.

Sanders, S., Jacobson, J.M. and Ting, L. (2005), Reactions of Mental Health Social Workers Following a Client Suicide or Attempt: A Qualitative Investigation, *Omega-Journal of Death and Dying.*

Suresh Kumar, P.N. (2004), An Analysis of Suicide Attempters Versus Completers in Kerala, *Indian Journal of Psychiatry,* 2004, 46(2).

Magazines

Bhonsle, M.R. (2004), Psychotherapy—A crying need for counselling, *Life Positive* retrieved from http://www.lifepositive.com/Mind/Psychotherapy/A_crying_need_for_counselling8 2004.asp retrieved 02.06.11

Datta, D. (2008), Teen Suicides. *India Today*, April 18, retrieved from http://indiatoday.digitaltoday.in/content_mail.php?option=com_content&name=print&id=7170

Mitra, N., Yasmeen, S., Roy, S., Patil, A. and Varoodhini, T. (2010), Student Counselling: an area of darkness. Educational World: *The Human Development Magazine*, retrieved from http://educationalworldonline.net/index.php/page-article-choice-more-id-2428

Newspapers

Chatterjee, S., Schools are Neglecting Counselling. *Indian Express*, June 28, 1999 http://www.indianexpress.com/ie/daily/19990628/ige28083.html

Rashid, T. (2005), Now, Schools to get their Own Mental Health Centres, *Indian Express*, August 2.

Emotional Awareness Initiative Launched for Adolescents, *The Hindu*, July 21, 2006. http://www.thehindu.com/2006/07/21/stories/2006072121900500.htm

Kurian, S., Making Sense of Sex Education in Schools: State Trends, *The Hindu*, September 25, 2007. http://www.thehindu.com/2007/09/25/stories/2007092555210500.htm

Delhi Government Schools—One Counsellor for 9000 students. *National Network of Education*, Delhi, June 17, 2009. http://www.indiaedunews.net/Delhi/Delhi_government_schools_one_counsellor_for_9000_students_8404/print.asp

Thomas, L. (2010), Bid to Identify Mental Health Problems of Students, *The Hindu*, March.

Lending a Helping Hand to Teenagers, *The Hindu*, December 10, 2009, p. 3, http://www.thehindu.com/2009/12/10/stories/2009121060420300.htm

George, S.E. (2002), The Last Resort, *The Hindu*, May, 12, 2002.

George, S.E., Suicide among school children in Kerala. *The Hindu*, May12, 2002.

Ending life, the easy way. *The Hindu*, June 10, 2002 http://www.hinduonnet.com/thehindu/mp/2002/06/10/stories/2002061000890200.htm

Sensitising Teachers to Adolescent Problems, *The Hindu*, July 7, 2006. http://www.thehindu.com/2006/07/07/stories/2006070717930500.htm

Counselling System for School Students, *The Hindu*, March 13, 2004. http://www.thehindu.com/2004/03/13/stories/2004031304200300

Walk the Talk with Teenager, *The Hindu*, November 16, 2006. http://www.thehindu.com/thehindu/mp/2006/11/16/stories/2006111601190300.htm

School Health Initiative, *Educationworldonline*, July 30, 2011, Delhi www.educationworldonline.net accessed on September 06, 2011.

Concern Over High Stress Level among Students, *The Hindu*, February 25, 2003.

Papers

Adeyinka, A.G. (2009), *Marriage and Family in Changing Society*. Ilesha: Wanday Press Publisher.

Bronstien, L.R. and Kelly, T.D. (1998, July), The Multi-dimensional approach to evaluating school linked services: A school social work and country public school partnership. *Social Work in Education,* Vol. 20, No. 3.

Bolu-steve, F.N. and Sanni, W.O. (2013, March), Influence of Family Background on the Academic Performance of Secondary School Students in Nigeria. *Life Psychologia,* Vol. 21, No. 1.

Reddy, E.V. (1995), Primary education in the web of poverty culture, Paper presented at the International Seminar on

School Effectiveness and Learning Achievement at Primary Stage, organized by National Council of Education Research and Training, July 17-19, 1995.

Reports

Barth, R.P., Lloyd, C., Christ, S. L., Chapman, M. V. and Dickinson, N. S. (2008), Child Welfare Worker Characteristics and Job Satisfaction: A National Study. *Social Work*, 53 (3).

Child Guidance Clinic, B.J. Wadia Hospital for Children, *Annual Reports, 1960-1965* (Mimeographed).

Ministry of Education: *Report of the Education Commission (1964-66)*, Education and National Development, Government of India.

Plowden Report (1967), *Children and Their Primary Schools*, London: HMSO.

Seebohm Report (1968), *Report of the Committee on Local Authority and Allied Personal Social Services*, London: HMSO.

White House Conference on Child Health and Protection. Preliminary Committee Reports. New York: Century 1930.

Unpublished Monographs

Goyal, C.P. (1980), *A Resume of the Development of School Social Work Movement in Kashi Vidyapeeth*? (Unpublished Paper).

Kumar, M.L. (1989), *Attitude of Teacher and Students Towards School Social Work Program*. Unpublished M.Phil. Dissertation submitted to Department of Social Work, Jamia Millia Islamia University.

Web Sources

Adams, A. (1996), *Even basic needs of young are not met*, Retrieved from http://tc.education. pitt.edu/library/SelfEsteem

Adela, C. Timmons, and Gayla, Margolin. (2014 Oct), Family Conflict, Mood, and Adolescents' Daily School Problems: Moderating Roles of Internalizing and Externalizing Symptoms. Retrieved on November 2014 from http://onlinelibrary.wiley.com/doi/10.1111/cdev.12300/abstract

Bhatnagar, A., (2012 May), The challenges that Indian teachers face when seeking employment at international schools and how to overcome them. Retrieved on May 10, 2015 from http://teacherhorizonsblog.com/2012/05/08/the-challenges-that-indian-teachers-face-when-seeking-employment-at-international-schools-and-how-to-overcome-them/

Catalano, R.F., Haggerty, K.P., Oesterle, S., Fleming, C.B., Hawkins, J.D., (2004 Oct), The Importance of Bonding to School for Healthy Development: Findings from the Social Development Research Group. *Journal of School Health*. Retrieved on January 2015, from https://www.researchgate.net/profile/Charles_ Fleming/publication/8222777_The_Importance_of_Bonding_to_School_for_Healthy_Development_Findings_from_the_Social_ Development_Research_Group/links/02bfe 510bf651ad7ae000000.pdf

Delhi Directorate of Education. New Delhi: Ministry of Education. Retrieved From https://en.wikipedia.org/wiki/Delhi_Directorate_of_Education

Dinesh, S. (2011), Prevalence of Stress Among School Children in Kerala, International Society for Analytical and Molecular Morphology. Retrieved on June 28, 2011 from http://www.isamm.org/prevalence-of-stress-among-school-children-in-kerala.htm

Kelly, M.S., Berzin, S.C., Frey, A., Alvarez, M., Shaffer, G., O'Brien, K. (2010 March), The State of School Social Work: Findings from the National School Social Work Survey. *School Mental Health*, 10.1007/s12310-010-9034-5. Retrieved from http://www.academia.edu/227460/The_State_of_School_Social_Work_Findings_from_the_ National_School_Social_Work_Survey

Linking School Social Work to Student Achievement. Wisconsin: Wisconsin Department of Public Instruction. Retrieved from http://dpi.wi.gov/sspw/socialwork.html#linking%20school%20social%20work%20to%20student%20achievement

Municipal Corporation of Delhi (MCD), Retrieved from https://en.wikipedia.org/wiki/Municipal_Corporation_of_Delhi

Rebecca, M. Ryan, Amy Claessens, and Anna, J. Markowitz, (2014), Associations Between Family Structure Change and

Child Behaviour Problems: The Moderating Effect of Family Income. Retrieved from http://onlinelibrary.wiley.com/doi/10.1111/cdev.12283/abstract

Roberts, G.A. (2007), The effect of extracurricular activity participation in the relationship between parent involvement and academic performance in a sample of third grade children. *UT Electronic Theses and Dissertations*. Retrieved from https://www.lib.utexas.edu/etd/d/2007/robertsg11186/robertsg11186.pdf

Roles of the School Social Worker, Wisconsin: Wisconsin Department of Public Instruction. Retrieved From http://dpi.wi.gov/sspw/socialwork.html#school%20social%20work%20roles

Saxton, J. (2000), Investment in Education: Private and Public Returns. Retrieved from http://www.house.gov/jec/educ.pdf

Suresh Kumar P.N. (2004), Current Research in Suicide in India. IMA Academy of Medical Specialties Kerala State Chapter. Retrieved on June 25, 2011, from http://www.manasikarogyam.com/index.php/files/category/6-english- books?download=Asuicide-prevention-manual-for-primary-care-givers&usg=AFQjCNF78LZcpsG3zG8-XRFJFUGGNARb8w

Usaj, K., Shine, J.K., Mandlawitz, M. (2009), Response to Intervention: New Roles for School Social Workers, *School Social Work Association of America,* Retrieved on August 19, 2009, from http://www.wisconsinpbisnetwork.org/assets/files/2012%20Conference/Session%20Material/Roles_School_Social_Workers_RTI.pdf

Index